Playing from the Heart

Playing from the Heart

Roger Crawford and Michael Bowker

Prima Publishing
P.O. Box 1260BK
Rocklin, CA 95677
(916) 632-4400

PRIMA PUBLISHING and colophon are registered trademarks of Prima Communications, Inc.

Library of Congress Cataloging-in-Publication Data

Crawford, Roger.
    Playing from the heart: a portrait in courage /
Roger W. Crawford
  II, Michael Bowker.–Rev.
        p.   cm.
     Includes index.
     ISBN 0-7615-0440-0
     1. Crawford, Roger. 2. Tennis players–
United States–Biography. 3. Physically handicapped–
United States–Biography. I. Bowker, Michael. II. Title.
  GV994.C73A3   1997
  796.342'092–dc21
   [B]   97-26575
                                         CIP

97 98 99 00 01 AA 10 9 8 7 6 5 4 3 2 1

Printed in the United States of America

How to Order
Single copies may be ordered from Prima Publishing,
P.O. Box 1260BK, Rocklin, CA 95677;
telephone (916) 632-4400. Quantity discounts are
also available. On your letterhead, include information
concerning the intended use of the books and
the number of books you wish to purchase.

Visit us online at www.primapublishing.com

*This book is dedicated to all the people
in my life who told me I could be somebody.*

Prologue

In a world that cherishes physical perfection, I've accepted that I am, and always will be, different. This uniqueness has shaped my life and outlook in a profound way. I've learned that there is much in our lives we cannot change, so we must strive to change what we can. Though handicaps are often out of our control, we *can* control our beliefs; therefore, we should embrace the power of choice to seek out and draw strength from the good and positive.

People often ask me what the cause of my physical challenge is. There is no definite answer; however, I've learned that the reason for a handicap is not as important as how we choose to handle the result. Here is the reality of my life and yours: Setbacks are often the difference between where you are and where you want to be.

Much has occurred in my life since the initial release of *Playing from the Heart*. I would like to express my gratitude to the hundreds of corporations, associations, and school districts that have given me the privilege of sharing my message with them. My travels have taken me to all 50 states and 17 foreign countries, and these experiences have given me memorable opportunities that few individuals ever encounter. I have observed peak performers—many of whom have become valued friends. Through this interaction, I have identified critical success factors that I believe are essential for both personal and professional success.

The highlight of my life occurred on April 24, 1992, when our daughter, Alexa Marie Crawford, was born. Fatherhood has enriched my life in ways I never thought possible. Alexa has shown me that children are our best teachers, and she's made me realize that I have as much to learn from her as she has to learn from me.

These learning experiences have inspired me to write "Second Serves" for the end of selected chapters. I hope you will find these principles useful in increasing your effectiveness in life and work. I feel honored to have the opportunity to share a little of my life with you.

Contents

1 The Imperfect Baby 1
2 My First Day of School 13
3 Gifts My Parents Gave Me 25
4 Touchdown! 33
5 What a Racket! 41
6 Making the Team 51
7 Fitting In 65
8 My First Dance 79
9 Learning to Drive 89
10 Apartment 101: Making the Grade at Loyola 99
11 A Leg Up on "Good Morning America" 115
12 Toward an Uncertain Future 129
13 She Said "Yes"! 149
14 The Power of Prayer 165
15 The Truth Ain't Hard to Remember 169
16 Miss Liberty 181
17 The Luckiest Man in the World 189

Chapter One

The Imperfect Baby

Carol and Roger Crawford were a happy young couple with a future. Carol, 23 years old, bright and attractive, had been a top student and beauty queen in their hometown of Canton, Ohio. Roger, 24 years old and six feet tall with a chest like a whiskey barrel, had been a baseball star in high school and at Duke University, where he gained undergraduate degrees in psychology and business.

Carol and Roger were like two sides of the same coin. She was gentle and nurturing, while he was decisive and ambitious. She was quiet and shy, he was outgoing and strong-willed. They had dated since they were 14 years old, but they held off getting married until Roger graduated from Duke. They believed if their love was true, it would survive Roger's college years. Shortly after he graduated in 1958 they were married.

Roger played semi-professional baseball for a season in 1959, but injuries cut short his dreams of glory. The following year he landed a job as a broker with the Associate Investment Corp. in South Bend, Indiana. Carol went to work as a secretary. In the evenings, after work, they liked to take long leisurely walks and talk about the family they wanted.

In February of 1960, Carol came back from her doctor bursting with news. She was going to have a baby! It was due in October. They made all the usual preparations; shopping for the crib and cradle, baby clothes and bottles, and they even bought a pair of little leather shoes for the baby.

Sonograms hadn't yet been perfected, so there was no way to find out the baby's sex, or to determine whether it was developing properly. But there was no reason to think otherwise. Carol's doctor said she was perfectly healthy and the pregnancy progressed normally throughout the summer.

When Carol went into labor in early October, everything seemed fine, except that she had a lot of early pain. Roger drove her to Marymount Hospital in downtown Bedford, but as was the custom in those days, he was not allowed beyond the waiting room. The doctors told him to go home, he would be called when the baby arrived.

The labor progressed normally. The doctors had given Carol a strong local anesthetic, which masked her pain. The nurses and doctors were talking steadily throughout the labor, up to the moment the baby came into the world. Carol was a little woozy from the anesthetic, but when the baby was born, she felt something was wrong. All the conversation had suddenly stopped. She knew the baby was alive because she could hear its small gurgling noises. Then the baby was whisked away and there was only an eerie silence. Carol didn't even know if she had a boy or a girl.

"Can I hold my baby?" she managed to ask.

The doctor walked up and stood stiffly by her side.

"Your baby has a number of problems," he said in a low voice. "There isn't anything we can do." He kept talking but through her anesthetic fog, Carol couldn't understand what he was saying. What was wrong with her baby? All she could make out was something about a hand—was there something wrong with the baby's hand?

Finally, a nurse brought the baby to Carol and she held her son for the first time. The anesthesia was still strong and she wasn't sure if she was hallucinating. The baby seemed to have no hands at all, just forearms that came to a point, and his legs were shortened and his feet terribly misshapen. Everything seemed crazy, nothing made sense. All she wanted to do was hug her baby tight before the nurse took him away again. Before she could form the words to ask questions about her son, a nurse took the baby and everyone left the room. The last nurse turned from the door, leaned over the bed, and hugged Carol.

"You're very brave," the nurse said, choking back her tears.

For two hours Carol laid in her bed alone. Occasionally a nurse would stop by on rounds, but none of them would tell her anything about her son, or her husband. Lying on her back she began to cry, silently, until her ears flooded with tears and the pillows were soaked. One of the most glorious events of one's life, the birth of a baby, had turned into a nightmare. Still the doctors refused to let her see her son again, or tell her what was happening. Later, Carol found out the doctors were waiting until Roger arrived at the hospital. But they didn't even phone Roger until they had done a battery of tests on the baby to determine the scope of his deformities.

Three hours after their son was born, Roger was allowed into the nursery. The front of the maternity ward was full of healthy, pink babies, bundled up behind an observation window. The nurse led Roger past these babies to a dimly lit room in the back, where his son lay, swaddled in blankets. The doctors had made sure to cover the baby's hands and legs so the other parents wouldn't become upset. The nurse slowly unwrapped the baby. The doctors had warned Roger that the baby wasn't "normal," but he wasn't prepared for what he saw. His son had a thumb-like projection extending directly out of his right forearm and a thumb and finger growing out of his left forearm. The baby had no palms. His arms and legs were shortened and he only had three toes on his shrunken right foot. The baby's withered left leg was folded beneath him.

Roger felt that the world had closed in on him. Surely this couldn't be happening—not to his baby! He tried to listen as the doctor explained. The baby suffered from *ectrodactylism*, a birth defect that affects 1 out of every 90,000 children born in the United States. The deformity isn't thought to be hereditary, but doctors do not know the cause. The baby had just been caught in the warp of random chance and there wasn't anything anybody could do about it.

The doctor gently told Roger that his son would never be able to walk and probably would never be able to care for himself. Then he shook hands with Roger and wished him good luck.

≥●

My parents had not yet picked out a name for me, but after my birth they decided to name me after my father — and so I became Roger William Crawford II. They chose that name to show me that they were proud of me and that they wanted me very much. When I was a child, I didn't like the name because everybody called me "Little Rog" when I wanted to be "Big Rog." It wasn't until I was older that I began to appreciate what they had done for me by giving me my father's name.

One of the toughest things my parents had to do when they took me home was to repeat the story of my birth to each member of the family.

Mom and Dad tried to keep very busy during the months after I was born — Dad with his new job and Mom, who had quit her job as a secretary, taking care of me. Staying active was a good tonic for both of them, but they still went through very rough times. A high percentage of marriages break up whenever a child is born with a severe birth defect. Dealing with normal children is difficult enough, but having a child that has special needs can create extra stress on a relationship. However, my parents grew to love each other even more in those painful days and they extended that love to me.

My mom now admits that she cried almost daily, whenever she thought about how I would ever be able to hold anyone's hand or feared that even the fingers I had wouldn't grow properly. My father, too, spent many sleepless nights fearing for my future. Would I ever be able to take care of myself?... Would I ever find a career?... A wife?

Through this, my parents never became bitter. My mother insists that she never felt anger over my birth defects, or asked, "Why me?"

The hardest part of all, though, were other people's reactions to me. My parents still tell stories about the time they took me along on a vacation to Florida when I was an infant. We went to the beach almost every day and they always dressed me in little shorts—they never attempted to hide my hands or legs. Even after 28 years, they still remember the faces of the couples who came by and peered into my stroller, and the smiles that quickly faded when they saw my hands and legs. One man's beaming face suddenly turned to stone. "Oh! Too bad," was all he said before he walked abruptly away.

My parents continued to explore medical options for me, and when I was two years old they were referred to a leading orthopedic surgeon in Cincinnati, Ohio. They were optimistic that surgery could help expand my physical capabilities. The doctor took a series of x-rays, and told my parents to prepare for bad news. He informed them that there was no fibula in my left leg and the tibia and fibula in my right leg were partially fused at my ankle, which would cause me trouble when I walked. He predicted that I would never lead a normal life. My parents walked slowly to their car. They were stunned and sat in the car for a moment. Then Dad slammed his hand on the dashboard and said he wouldn't accept the doctor's prognosis. Shortly afterwards, my parents sought advice from the doctors at the Shriners Hospital in Chicago.

Perhaps the most difficult psychological obstacles my parents faced were the feelings of guilt that would enter their thoughts during unguarded moments. "Was I to blame for my son's deformities? Could I have prevented them, somehow?" And worst of all, "Am I being punished for something I did?" As rational, intelligent people, they knew that my problems were the result of random chance and that they were in no way responsible. They hadn't taken any drugs (I wasn't a thalidomide baby). My mother didn't drink or smoke. It was just bad luck. But the questions still lingered, especially for Mom. It wasn't until five years later, when my brother Brian was born with ten perfect fingers and ten perfect toes, that she got over her guilt. The decision to have a second child was not an easy one. My parents had seen a number of doctors and had taken a number of chromosomal tests. Doctors at the Shriners Hospital in Chicago did a search of our family's medical history, and after looking at all the data, determined that the chances were very good that my parents' next baby would be perfectly normal.

In the months prior to Brian's birth, when I was five years old, my parents had to make yet another tough decision. It was becoming apparent that my left leg was withering and it was getting more difficult for me to walk. My left leg was shorter than my right and my left foot actually pointed straight toward the ground when I was standing up. The leg slouched out to the right so I walked with a pronounced limp. The foot was absolutely useless and I had to wear a cumbersome metal brace called a *walking caliber*.

My father spent hours every day massaging my legs to help them grow straight and to strengthen them. But I couldn't walk without limping and I couldn't run, so my parents were encouraged when the doctors at the Shriners Hospital told them about a new surgical procedure that might be able to help me. The procedure was called *disarticulation* and it involved amputating my left foot at the ankle bone. I would have to wear a prosthesis for the rest of my life, but the doctors said with the advancements in prosthetic devices there was a chance I could learn to walk and maybe even run in a limited way. But my parents still agonized over the idea of amputating part of my leg. The other two options included doing nothing, leaving me to wear a brace and a lift on my left foot for the rest of my life; or another surgery where doctors would implant a pin in my right leg to stunt its growth. This would keep my legs approximately the same size, but would also have prevented me from growing over five feet tall.

None of the options were easy and Mom especially had a difficult time deciding. Dad was for the disarticulation operation because he had dreamed of watching me run like the other kids and this seemed to be my only chance. When my parents asked me what I wanted to do, I said I wasn't sure, until they told me one of the operations might enable me to run with the other children. Then my eyes lit up and I told them I wanted to have it done right away.

The operation and rehabilitation proved difficult. Chicago is several hours away by car from Bedford, and was too far for Mom to drive, since she was in her third trimester with Brian. Dad tried to see me whenever he could. He drove up most weekends, which gave him no time to relax from his high-pressure job.

Although I was excited about the prospects of being able to run, I was very lonely in the hospital. I had been there before, a couple times a year, when my parents took me to "Clinic Day." I always hated Clinic Day, when hundreds of handicapped children would come to the hospital for general tests and check-ups. It was hard for me to see all the kids missing arms or legs, or wearing braces, because I felt sad for them. I never looked at myself as limited, but on Clinic Day the truth became unavoidable — I was there with the rest of these kids because we were all handicapped.

The hospital was a huge, sterile place that seemed a million miles from home. There were other children on the floor, though, and the nurses did their best to keep us busy. I became fast friends with a boy my age named Sam, who was from Louisville, Kentucky. Sam was born with no legs, but that didn't stop him. Sam was athletic — we'd play soccer in the playroom and he would raise up on his hands and "kick" the ball by swinging his torso. We shared our dreams of becoming professional athletes — Sam wanted to be a professional football player when he grew up. Despite his physical problems, Sam was one of the happiest kids I ever knew. He always had a good word for everybody and he organized games for all the children to play. When the nurses weren't around, we would climb into the wheelchairs and race down the halls, bashing into flower pots and anything else that got in our paths. Although Sam and I were wonderful friends during the four months we were in the hospital together, we lost touch after that. I saw him only once again at a Clinic Day, three years later. Sam was in a wheelchair and he was the same old Sam — doing wheelies down the corridors with the nurses in hot pursuit. I often wonder what ever happened to him, though with his spirit, I'm sure he's made a great success out of his life.

In spite of friends like Sam, I got terribly lonesome at night and would cry myself to sleep. I was mad at my parents for leaving me, and although I knew I was supposed to have an operation, I wasn't sure exactly what that meant. I just knew that I had been left alone in this huge hospital and I didn't like it.

The operation itself took several hours. The doctors amputated my left foot and sewed some of the tougher skin from my foot around the bottom of the ankle bone. At the same time, they took the Achilles tendon from my ankle and surgically implanted it in my left hand, between my fingers and along my wrist area. That operation was an important one, as well, because it allowed me to pinch my fingers together. For the first time, I could use my fingers to grasp an object.

I don't remember any pain from the operation itself, but the rehabilitation process was difficult. The doctors were concerned that the skin on the bottom of my stump wouldn't be tough enough to endure the rigors of walking in a prosthesis, so they made me bang the bottom of my leg against a piece of leather to toughen the skin. It hurt, but the nurses did their best to coax me to do it each day by telling me stories about how I would be able to walk and run like other children. I always did my exercises, but I'll never forget the pain and the dread I felt when I entered the exercise room and saw that old piece of leather waiting for me.

One day, a nurse came in with my first artificial leg. It was made of wood and it had a little rubber foot on the end. (Since the early 1960s, prosthesis technology has evolved dramatically. Most of my artificial legs—I've had 15 of them so far—were made of fiberglass. However, the newest artificial legs are made of a composite of graphite, fiberglass, and ceramics, which, ironically, are the same materials from which they make new tennis rackets.)

My first little wooden leg was open at the top and the stump of my leg fit right in it. I was so excited I grabbed it out of the nurse's hand, slid it on, and ran down the hall as fast as I could. It was the first time in my life I had ever run. The nurse scurried after me screaming, "You can't do that, you can't do that!" But I could and I did. I led her on a merry chase around the halls, hollering at the other little kids at the top of my lungs to watch me run. By the time the nurse caught up with me, my leg was bleeding and sore, but I was laughing and shouting. I could run!

I couldn't wait to show my parents. They flew to Chicago soon after Brian was born. When they finally came through the doorway of the lobby I yelled, "Mommy, I can run!" and I took off as fast as I could go down the hallway. Both of my parents had tears streaming down their faces when I reached them. They picked me up and hugged me for what seemed like an eternity. It had been a long and terrible four months, but now it was over. I could go home. And now I could run. *I could run!*

Second Serve

Handicaps can only disable us if we let them. This is true not only of physical challenges, but of emotional and intellectual ones as well. You see, we all have different abilities, and once we accept them we will begin to see new ways of looking at ourselves and the world around us. I believe that real and lasting limitations are created in our minds, not in our bodies. We must accept ourselves and do the best we can with our unique talents and abilities.

As you read this book you'll see that the essence of my life is not much different from yours. We all face adversity and challenges— it just so happens that mine are visible.

Chapter Two

My First Day of School

I wore shorts on my first day of school at the Royal View Elementary School in Willowick, Ohio, a suburb of Cleveland. My parents had decided that if I was going to survive in the able-bodied world, it was best to get the hard knocks out of the way as soon as possible. They felt it was better for the kids to see my handicaps right away. I suppose these days they'd call what my parents did "mainstreaming." In my case, they tossed me into the main part of the stream and said, "Okay, Roger, swim!"

There were special schools for children who were different, including physically challenged kids. The schools had different teachers, a different curriculum (although the kids were physically, not mentally, handicapped), and the children even rode on different school buses. The idea was that a physically handicapped child just couldn't keep up. My parents thought that for me, these special schools would create a disabling, not enabling, atmosphere—and I will always be thankful for that decision. Growing up in public schools allowed me to live and succeed in the mainstream, even though sometimes it wasn't easy.

In those days, there wasn't much sensitivity toward physically handicapped people, even in schools. My first grade teacher always referred to me in conversations as "the handicapped one," even when I was within earshot. The first time I heard her say that, I told her, "No, I'm not, I'm Roger." My parents had never used the words "handicapped" or "disabled" when they referred to me and I wasn't sure what the words meant.

For the most part, the other kids at school treated me as an oddity. They weren't mean or rude, but they were curious. I remember them looking at me with long stares and a few of them asked me what had happened to my hands. My parents had prepared me for their questions, though.

"Tell them, that was the way you were born," my mother told me. And that's just what I said. "That's the way I was born," I said over and over again. Most of the children were content with that answer, but a few couldn't resist teasing me. "Lobster hands" quickly became my nickname, although in some more creative corners I was known as "Three Fingered Louie."

My parents had prepared me for this, too. I remember Mom saying, "If someone makes fun of you because of the way you look on the outside, that's their handicap on the inside." I wore this wisdom like a suit of armor and when someone made fun of me, I would tell them they had a handicap on the inside and that shut them right up. It wasn't long before most of the teasing stopped. Of course, the curious stares never have.

Of all the things my parents had to endure because I was different, the taunting of the other children was the toughest. Kids can be merciless and I was an easy target. Since I was at the bottom of the physical pecking order, I was easy prey to bullies, although later, when I received my artificial leg, I developed a pretty mean kick that the bullies came to respect. But occasionally, I came home bloodied and bruised and I know that caused far more pain for my parents than it did for me. It would have been much easier for them to have put me in a special education school where I would have been safe from that kind of harm.

The shorts were my dad's idea. He's always operated on the principle that if you have a problem, confront it right away because problems have a way of growing if you don't tend to them. It's not always the easiest way, he'd say, but in the long run, it's the best way. Although putting your one-legged child in shorts on the first day of school might seem a bit harsh to some people, it turned out to be the best way for me in the long run.

That first day was tough, though. I can remember coming home after school, having been called "lobster hands" all day, and crying buckets. It was my harshest experience with rejection and ridicule. But my dad told me the worst part was over now, the kids had gotten a good look at my handicap—and he was right.

There were a few hitches along the way. For example, because of the way my hands were formed, I couldn't unbuckle or unzip my pants. If you are fully equipped physically, you probably never gave it much thought. But if you can't do it—and if you are too embarrassed to tell anybody about it, as I was—not being able to unbuckle or unzip your pants can pose a very real problem.

I went to school, all day every day, without ever going to the bathroom. Let me tell you, some of those days got mighty long. At lunch time, when all the other kids would be drinking their milk, I traded mine away. I also stayed away from the water fountain so I could make it through the day. Even at that, I always had to sprint home after school. By the end of that first year, I had the best trained bladder at Royal View Elementary. I finally told my parents about the problem and my dad said he thought he could fix things for me. He tied a loop of string on my zipper tab, big enough so I could slip the small finger on my left hand inside the loop and pull the zipper up or down. What a relief! Now I could use the bathroom, just like the other kids! As far as I was concerned, that invention ranked right up there with the light bulb and sliced bread.

Many of my early experiences were similar to any child's while growing up, but there were times when I was inevitably singled out. For example, one day my second grade teacher, Mr. Cross, decided we would all do hand prints for our parents. Mr. Cross was a slightly built man, with brown hair always parted meticulously on one side, and his clothes were neat as a pin. He was just out of graduate school and he was totally devoted to his students. Whenever he talked to us, he'd lean down close to our faces and speak softly. He was everybody's favorite teacher.

But as soon as Mr. Cross announced we were going to make hand prints, the entire class turned and looked at me to see what I was going to do. This time, no armor could save me—I was mortified. I jumped up and ran out of the room as fast as I could. I ran down a big hallway and was headed outside when Mr. Cross caught up to me.

"Roger!" he shouted. "I want you to come back into the classroom. I want you to do the hand prints like everybody else."

I told him I couldn't because I was handicapped. (In the past year I had learned the meaning of the word from my classmates and teachers.)

"Nonsense!" Mr. Cross boomed in a big voice that belied his jockey-like build. "You're not handicapped, you're Roger. You're my student and my students learn they are only handicapped when they don't do the best they can." He made me take my hands out of my pockets and walked me back to the classroom. He stayed by my side and helped me put my fingers in the ink and make the prints. He told me I was special, and no one had ever told me that before, except my family. I signed the prints, "Love, Roger," and gave them to my parents, who hung them in the greatest gallery in the world, on the Crawford refrigerator.

As I grew up, I began to discover that my physical differences had some benefits. For example, I could wrap my finger around a dirt clod and whip it with my arm through the air with amazing speed and accuracy. This gave me a certain stature in the neighborhood, among the boys anyway. I remember walking through an abandoned field one day when I met up with a group of boys, whose leader was a short, stocky Italian kid named Donnie Ponzoni. Donnie was built solidly and low to the ground and even at six years old he looked like he needed a shave.

   Donnie was with a group of tough boys and they started making fun of me. We were in the middle of the field and I was outnumbered, but I lost my temper at their taunting. I picked up some dirt clods and pinged a couple of them. My aim was deadly accurate and the clods stung when they landed, so the boys dove for cover. The battle raged for several minutes — I had them pinned down and was having a great time when they decided they had had enough. After a truce was declared, they all trooped over to inspect my hands and my throwing technique. Donnie and I became fast friends after that. He liked me because of my prowess as a dirt clod warrior and I liked him because his legs were so short his mother had to roll up his trouser legs, just like my mother had to do for me. Donnie was my first friend and he ultimately played an important part in helping me become "mainstreamed."

   I was still the butt of a lot of jokes in my early school years, but I remember one day when a new kid came to school. I passed him in the hall and he began to make fun of my hands. Suddenly, Donnie Ponzoni and another boy appeared at my side and warned the new kid: "Shut up, or else!" because I was their friend. I'll never forget that moment as long as I live. It was the first time anybody outside of my family ever stuck up for me and it felt good.

But even my friends couldn't save me from the twin terrors of gym class — high jumping and square dancing. During the cooler days of fall and winter I wore long pants and since I did not walk with a limp, very few of the children and none of the teachers knew I had an artificial leg. When spring came, our teacher, Mrs. Wiseman, moved our gym class outside — to the high jump pit.

She lined us up and one by one the kids took their turns trying to leap over the high jump bar. This was in the days before the Fosbury Flop was popularized, and most of the kids were trying to scissor jump their way over the bar, something I absolutely could not do. When it came my turn, I panicked. I just couldn't do it. I wouldn't tell Mrs. Wiseman why I couldn't and before long she became extremely frustrated and sent me straight to the principal's office. The principal was very stern and looked me right in the eye.

"Why won't you high jump?" he demanded. I was quiet for a moment, then I answered him.

"I only have one leg, sir." I showed him my artificial leg and I started to cry. Pretty soon the whole room was crying — me, the principal, Mrs. Wiseman, and even the secretary. We must have been quite a sight.

Although my high jumping career had come to a halt, later I had to do something that was even worse — square dance. Square dancing, of course, involved holding hands with a girl, which was tough enough for any small boy. For me, it was a nightmare.

Sure enough, when I finally got up enough nerve to try it, one girl shouted—"I'm not going to hold *his* hands!" I was devastated. I ran out of the gym, down the hall, and ended up back in the principal's office. I was crying so hard my parents had to come to school and take me home. This was one time that instead of being "mainstreamed" I sank to the bottom like the proverbial stone.

I was so crushed by the little girl's rejection that I wanted to quit and transfer to the special education school. There, all the kids had some kind of physical inconvenience and I wouldn't be singled out as much. But my parents would have none of it. They talked to me for hours about the need to adapt in life and how the only failure was in not trying. I'm not sure I understood what all their words meant then, but I did feel the love and support they gave me and I finally agreed to go back to school.

One of the first things the school administrators did when I returned was to send me to the school psychologist. The schools—and society at large—were beginning to gain an awareness of handicapped people, but the first steps were very clumsy. The first thing the psychologist asked me was whether I ever felt like not living, which was a nice way of asking whether I had ever felt like committing suicide. The prevailing attitude at the time was that if you were physically challenged you were probably depressed and perhaps suicidal. I answered truthfully, and said no.

I don't remember many of the other questions she asked me, or the tests I had to take, but I remember I liked her very much. She was young, tall, and gentle and I developed a crush on her. She had long blond hair and wore brightly colored miniskirts. I thought she was the most beautiful person in the world. On the days that I was to see her I would sneak into my parents' room and load up on my dad's Old Spice. I'd slick my hair back so I looked real cool and I'd be on pins and needles the entire day of my session.

Physically-challenged people have one of the highest rates of alcoholism and drug dependency of any specialized group in America. Lack of self esteem can lead to self-destructive behavior. I believe that part of the problem is how people who are "different" are treated in our society. They are often stared at, sometimes ridiculed and often excluded from participating in the rituals of society, like dating or sports.

One reason for this discrimination is that when able-bodied people see someone with hands like mine, or someone in a wheelchair, or someone who's blind, they are confronted with the fragility of life. Handicapped people may as well wear a big sign around their necks saying, "This could be you!"

Television hasn't helped. We're constantly bombarded with perfect-looking people on TV shows and commercials. If you don't fit that mold — if you're not a certain weight, don't look and smell a certain way — then you're not okay. How many handicapped people do you see on TV? Very few. *Yet at least one out of every ten people in the United States has a physical disability.*

I'm hopeful this situation will improve. The news media and movies like "Mask," "Children of a Lesser God," and "The Other Side of the Mountain" have helped sensitize viewers to the special needs of the physically challenged. But we still have a long way to go. I wish you could walk with me some time down a crowded mall when I'm wearing shorts. People always stare because of what I look like on the outside and I have to admit that deep down the stares hurt.

My first attempt to seek acceptance was becoming the class clown. I made wisecracks, often at the expense of my own physical shortcomings, and if there was a practical joke to be played — a tack to be placed on the teacher's chair — I was the perpetrator.

Later, sports became a more productive outlet. Being good at athletics was a great equalizer for me — people accepted me when I excelled and my self esteem would shoot up like a hot stock in a bull market. But that's another chapter.

There is a flip side to this problem of lack of self esteem, of course. If society has a duty to become sensitive to the needs of the physically challenged, people like me have a duty to themselves to become strong enough to make it through. I firmly believe in what my father taught me: confront your problems, learn what you can do and what you can't do, then do what you can do to the best of your ability. Of course, you don't have to be handicapped to benefit from this wisdom.

But no matter how well you prepare, life can often take an unexpected turn. That's especially true when you're eight. About the time I finally gained acceptance from my classmates at Royal View Elementary, my father was offered a new job with the Kaiser Aluminum Corporation in Ravenswood, a small rural town in the backwaters of West Virginia. When I learned we were going to move, I felt terrible.

Now I had to go through the first day of school routine all over again! I began to wonder what my new nicknames would be and how many times I would have to explain about my hands. I was going to miss Donnie Ponzoni and my gang of friends; who knew what type of kids were in West Virginia!

I said a tearful goodbye to Donnie and our old home in Ohio and we drove south to the Allegheny Mountains and Ravenswood (population 3,000). The community was so small that it didn't take long for me to realize I was the only handicapped kid in the entire town. As summer came to an end, I began to get nervous about starting school. But just before classes started, Carolyn Miller, a reporter for the local town paper, the *Ravenswood News*, heard about me and asked for an interview. My parents agreed, and Carolyn came over to our house and we spent a pleasant afternoon together. She wrote a wonderful article about me that explained all about my handicaps. The paper also ran a picture of me with a basketball, shooting a jump shot. Since everybody in town read the *News*, it saved me from having to explain to all the kids about my hands. In fact, after the article appeared, a lot of our neighbors made a point of coming over and introducing themselves. It was great for my parents because it made them feel welcome in the community. By the time school started, I was somewhat of a local celebrity and my first day of school was a breeze.

Chapter Three

Gifts My Parents Gave Me

When I was ten, a boy moved into our neighborhood (I'll call him Tommy, although that's not his real name), who was born missing an arm and a leg. I remember Tommy's parents talking to mine about his problems and it was apparent they were devastated. I rarely saw Tommy because he went to the special education schools and he never played outside in the neighborhood parks, where I always played with the other kids. When I would see him, he'd invariably keep his face to the ground and would never say a word.

One summer it got very hot and Mom began taking me to the public swimming pool. I used to get a lot of stares with my swimming trunks and artificial leg. At first, I used to swim with my artificial leg on, but as I got bolder, I would take it off and jump in. The kids used to tease me—good-naturedly—about only being able to swim in circles without my leg.

"Naw," I told them. "I can swim straight all right, but it sure cramps my diving style." The kids laughed and within a couple of weeks I was just part of the gang at the swimming pool.

One day, as my mother and I were walking back from the public pool, I heard the sounds of construction behind the fence at Tommy's house. I asked Mom what was going on and she told me that Tommy's parents were building him a private swimming pool. I then realized what my parents had done for me. Instead of hiding me behind a fence, they led me out into the real world and filled me with the belief that I belonged.

I've seen Tommy once or twice since then and although he is mentally sharp, he has had trouble functioning outside his protective wall. The very best gift my parents gave me was what they did *not* give me at all—a reason to hide.

My parents learned everything they could about handicapped children, but most of what they learned was through first-hand experience with me. My father knew no other handicapped people and my mother's only experience was enough to give her nightmares. When my mother was a child, a little neighbor girl, who was physically and mentally handicapped, was kept leashed to a tree in the front yard so she wouldn't wander into the nearby street. She would scream nonsensical words at my mother whenever she walked by.

My parents simply went by their instincts, and refused to treat me differently. But they paid a price for this. Once, when I was six years old, my mother and I were in the checkout line at the grocery store.

A pregnant woman was in line just in front of us and when she saw me, she raised a huge fuss. She thought my handicap was contagious. She was afraid her baby would catch what I had.

Other people, using their misguided religious beliefs as weapons, insinuated to my parents that they must have committed some horrible sin for this to have happened to me. As stupid and cutting as those kinds of remarks were, they were still easier for my parents to ignore than the persistent rumors about thalidomide.

As you may remember, thalidomide was a drug developed in West Germany to help curb morning sickness in expectant mothers. It was used extensively in Europe and to some extent in the United States and Canada from the mid 1950s until the early 1960s. Finally, it became horribly evident that thalidomide had a terrible side effect. It deformed the fetus. Thalidomide babies were often born with malformed hands and feet. Therefore, many people jumped to the false conclusion that I was a thalidomide baby. I can still remember one of the neighborhood boys telling me that my parents had taken drugs and that's why I was the way I was. Of course, this was not true.

My parents were all too aware that many people would assume thalidomide caused my handicaps. They knew the more they exposed me in public, the more icy disapproval they were going to have to endure. But they did it anyway because they believed it was the best thing for me. They taught me that love isn't always simple.

When I was seven years old, my dad used to play tackle football with me in our back yard. I'd put on the shoulder pads and helmet that my parents bought for me and Dad would toss me the ball and tell me to try to run past him. I'd turn on the speed and try to make a move or two on him and then — Whap! — he'd knock me flat. "Again!" he'd say, and we'd do it again. He wanted me to lose my fear of competing against able-bodied athletes. We'd talk while we played. "You're only as handicapped as you want to be," he'd intone over and over again.

If I came home complaining about having three fingers and one leg and half a foot, Dad would immediately remind me of the kids we saw on Clinic Day who didn't have any legs or arms, and he'd make me feel grateful for what I did have.

We'd often go fishing and camping. Our favorite fishing hole was a place called Turkey Foot Lake near Canton, Ohio. Mom would pack us a little picnic lunch and Grandpa, Dad, and I would sit on the shore and cast out for bass, walleye, and bluegill. Dad taught me how to use a fishing reel — I'd put my right finger on the side of the reel and crank like crazy. I always had trouble baiting the hook when we used worms, though, so I just stuck to using lures.

Like most kids, I sometimes felt my parents were a little too hard on me. If I got a B on my report card, my father wanted to know why it wasn't an A. My parents — my father especially — expected the very best out of me and he would tell me right away if I didn't live up to those expectations. He'd say, "It's better to aim at the stars, because even if you miss, the moon ain't bad."

Whenever I think of Mom, I think of the word "affectionate." She was and is absolutely constant in her devotion to her family. She told me over and over again that I had special gifts—that everyone had special gifts—and it was our job to develop those gifts as much as we could. She'd take me shopping, holding my hand the entire time. It made me feel like the most important person in the world.

She also helped me become a popular guy in the neighborhood because she made the best peanut butter cup cookies on the block. She'd criss-cross the top of them with a fork and when the aroma of freshly baked cookies began wafting around the neighborhood, the Crawford household suddenly became the center of attention.

Mom was the first person to tell me, "It's not the wrapping of a person that matters, it's the gift they have on the inside that counts."

I guess it was that philosophy that convinced my parents to risk having another child. The doctors had informed them there was no reason to believe their next child would be born handicapped. But even if the child were physically challenged, Mom and Dad felt it would be okay with them. When my brother, Brian, entered the world, the doctor told Mom that her new baby boy was a robust nine-pounder. "Nine pounds!" she gasped. "My gosh, we must have prayed too hard."

I can still remember the first time I saw baby brother Brian—Mom unwrapped him for me and there he was, naked, lying on a nursing blanket. I was six years old and I circled around him cautiously. I counted two arms, two legs, five fingers on each hand and five toes on each foot. "What's wrong with him?" I wanted to know.

ë⬥

As my brother got older, I became jealous of him. I was afraid that Dad would favor him because Brian could play baseball. Of course, that didn't happen. But I still resented that my brother could catch a ball in his baseball mitt while I had to catch it against my chest.

Brian, who later excelled in college and is now pursuing a professional baseball career, connected immediately with Dad through baseball. Brian could catch and throw and do all the things my dad loved to do — and I couldn't. It was frustrating that when my brother and I fought, he always won, even though I was six years older! The trouble was, I couldn't make a fist or grab him because of my hands. Luckily, before my jealousy could harden into a long-lasting resentment, I discovered tennis and became an athlete in my own right. Once I became secure in my abilities as a tennis player, I lost my jealousy toward Brian and now he has no greater fan.

Being my brother was no picnic either. When Brian was little, the kids used to tease him because of me. But he survived it, and he even got used to doing things like tying my shoes at school and helping me get those slippery worms on the hook when we went fishing. Later, he became popular with his friends when he brought them over after school and showed them my stash of artificial legs. I remember the kids saying, "Wow, those are really neat." They would strap on one of my legs and hobble around.

Later, when I began to succeed at tennis and to get a lot of attention, Brian had to deal with the fact that he wasn't different like I was—he was just like everybody else. I used to kid him that his handicap was that he didn't have one.

When I was 16 years old, I worked all summer as a department store clerk and saved the princely sum of $350. To me, that was a fortune and I thought it represented a great sacrifice. After all, working at the department store meant giving up days at the swimming pool, but I had something in mind. I wanted, more than anything, to buy a car. By the end of the summer, I had enough money to buy a used green Ford Fairlane with shiny moon rims, but there was one problem—I didn't have enough money to buy insurance. So, Dad made a deal with me. He promised to buy the insurance; in exchange, I had to keep up a B+ average in school. I was never a bad student in high school, but neither was I a standout. My heart and mind were into playing tennis and sometimes my school work was the worse off for it. Our deal had a catch (Dad's version of the fine print). If I didn't maintain my grades, he would cancel my insurance and sell my car. He would pay himself back the insurance money from the proceeds of the car sale and give the rest to me.

I got the car, then forgot our deal. My grades dropped and, true to his word and despite my pleadings, my dad sold the Fairlane. He took the money he had paid out in insurance and gave me the rest. I had about $125 left, about one-third of what the car cost.

I was shocked. I knew it was part of our bargain, but I still didn't believe he would actually go through with it. I should have known better. He was teaching me a lesson the best way he knew how. I was angry and even packed a little bag with some clothes and a toothbrush to run away from home, but I eventually cooled off. My grades remained high through the rest of my school years. I've never forgotten the importance of holding up my end of a contract.

Something my parents never did was to allow me to feel sorry for myself, or to take advantage of people because of my handicap. Once, I got into trouble because my school papers were continually late. I had to hold the pencil with both hands, and writing fatigued my fingers, so I couldn't write very fast. I explained that to Dad and asked him if he would write a note to my teachers, asking them for a two-day extension on my assignments. Instead, Dad made me start writing my papers two days early!

I never saw my parents cry about my handicaps. A few years ago I asked Dad about that. "We did cry," he said. "We just did it after you went to bed so you wouldn't see."

ॐ

Not long ago my parents appeared with me on the television show "People Are Talking" in San Francisco and they were asked, "If you had to give a word of advice for anybody in the audience on parenting, what would it be?" My parents conferred for a moment, then Dad answered. "I think the most important thing is to teach your kids how to walk — and then to let them walk away with a dream in their lives."

Chapter Four

Touchdown!

When I was 11 years old, I surprised a lot of people by making the Ravenswood Knickerbocker basketball team. (We called ourselves the "Knicks" after the New York Knickerbockers who had recently won the National Basketball Association championship.) Most people didn't think I would be able to play basketball, but my dad had hammered up a hoop and backboard in our backyard and even installed lights so I could shoot at night. I played so much I wore the leather right off my basketball.

Although I was short, I was a good shooter and was especially good at defense. Having only three fingers was a hindrance, but it did give me great hand speed. I became adept at flicking my hand in and stealing the ball while the other guy was dribbling.

By the time our season got underway, I was on the starting team. Our coach, a wonderful man named Ray Richey, affectionately called me his "power forward." Coach Richey always encouraged us, no matter how badly we played. We lost some games early, but as the season progressed, we blossomed under his guidance and became one of the better teams in the league. I loved basketball because through it I steadily gained the respect of the other boys. We found common ground — now we always had basketball to talk about. Most of them stopped thinking of me as the handicapped guy — I was Coach Richey's power forward.

I wasn't the star of our team, but I scored two or three baskets every game and I played good defense. By the end of the year, we had won our division and were slated to play for the league championship against the Hawks, a team that was heavily favored to win. By this time, Coach Richey had us believing in ourselves and we were determined to give the Hawks a run for their money.

On the day of the championship game, the gym was full of people — parents, teachers, and students. Some of the boys on our team were so nervous they put their jerseys on backwards.

The game was close from the beginning. We traded baskets and neither team could get more than two points ahead. We were ahead by two at the half, but the Hawks came back and took the lead going into the fourth quarter. Finally, with one minute left in the game, we tied the score. It was the Hawks' ball and the game was now on the line. The guy I was guarding brought the ball down court and I met him near the mid-court line. He was dribbling around looking for somebody to whom to pass when I whipped my hand in and slapped the ball loose. It bounced away and I pounced on it near the sideline. My man was now guarding me, so I put on my best spin moves trying to get away from him. But he stuck to me like glue, and I knew time was running out. I spun and spun and spun and finally I broke loose. I looked, and there was nobody between me and the basket! I dribbled as fast as I could and I beat everybody down court. I shot an easy layup, but to my horror, I missed. As luck would have it, the ball bounced right back into my hands. I shot it again—and missed again! From the stands, I could hear my Dad's big baritone voice yelling, "Go! Go!" So I grabbed my own rebound and put it back up. This time my aim was perfect and the ball snapped through the net.

I was thrilled and raced back down court. I looked for my teammates to celebrate with some high fives, but then I stopped short. Something was wrong. The guys on the Hawks' bench were going crazy, they were laughing, giving high fives, and falling all over each other. Meanwhile, our guys were looking at me as if I had just sprouted horns. Then it hit me. I had been shooting at the wrong basket! I had just scored two points for the Hawks!

My dad, I found out later, wasn't shouting, "Go! Go!" He was shouting, "No! No!"

Nobody scored another basket and we lost the game and the league championship by two points—the two points I had given the Hawks with my wrong-way goal.

I took a lot of ribbing about that basket from everybody in the entire school. At first, I cried and swore never to play basketball again, but as time went on, I found I had gained a kind of celebrity status at school. Being able to kid me gave some students, who otherwise were afraid to approach me, a reason to talk to me. As it turned out, I made a lot of new friends because of my wrong-way basket.

~❧

Dad always encouraged me to get involved with sports. Athletics had played a big part in his life. He had received a number of offers from big league teams after playing at Duke, before the leg injury cut his career short. He thought sports would be an ideal way for me to fit in with the other kids and to build my self esteem. But even beyond that, he figured the more I exercised my hands and legs, the more mobile I would be.

On winter nights, we'd toss a volleyball around inside as we watched television. He'd encourage me to catch the ball against my chest and throw it back to him. My mom deserves a lot of credit for putting up with us, because I broke a couple of her best lamps before I learned to throw accurately.

In some ways, my physical differences gave me an advantage in sports. I was much quicker with my hands than most kids because my hands weren't as big, nor my arms as long. Also, my right leg was very strong, since it often had to do the work of both my legs. As a result, when I was nine years old, I was the best tetherball and kickball player at school. That greatly boosted my popularity among the other kids. I learned early that succeeding in sports could give me something I desperately wanted — prestige in the able-bodied world.

Football was my favorite sport when I was growing up. My dad and I played a lot together in the back
yard and after being tackled by him, I wasn't afraid of
being hit by any of the kids in the Pop Warner
leagues. When I was 12 years old, I won a spot as the
starting left defensive end on a Ravenswood Pop
Warner League team. I liked playing defensive end
because one of my favorite players at the time was
Merlin Olsen, one of the "Fearsome Foursome" of the
Los Angeles Rams. When I played in my back yard, I
fantasized about lining up next to Merlin and the
other Rams as we became the Fearsome Fivesome.

We had a good Pop Warner team and won most
of our games. I got in on a lot of tackles, but more
than anything else, I wanted to score a touchdown. It
isn't easy for a defensive guy to do that, but it can be
done. My plan was to sack the quarterback and force
him to fumble. Then I would pounce on the ball and
run it back for a TD. I visualized that play every night
before a game, and finally, one day late in the season,
I got my chance to act out my plan.

The other team had the ball at midfield and it
was 3rd down and 15 yards to go. The enemy quarterback dropped back to pass. Usually, there was an
offensive lineman there to block me, but this time
there was nobody between me and the quarterback.
I rushed in, bent on knocking the ball loose. But my
plan was thwarted when our right defensive end beat
me to the punch. He belted the quarterback from the
side—and the ball popped straight up into my arms!
(Now that's what I call flexible planning.) I pinned it

against my chest and began to run as fast as I could down the sidelines. I could see my coach jumping wildly in the air, whirling his arms like a helicopter. I kept telling my legs to go faster, but as I neared the goal line, one of the guys from the other team caught up with me. At the 10-yard line he made his dive and grabbed me by the ankle — my left ankle. I tried to pull my leg away, but he hung on like a bulldog. I pulled and he pulled. Something had to give and it did — my artificial leg popped right off into the guy's arms! Meanwhile, I was still standing up. I didn't know what else to do so I started hopping toward the goal line. My would-be tackler just sat there looking at my artificial leg with a stunned look on his face. When I crossed the goal line, the referee ran over and threw both arms into the air. I knew what that meant.

Touchdown!

The argument that ensued may still be the only one of its kind ever to take place on the gridiron. The opposing team's coach was laughing, but he still asked for a ruling.

"How do I know?" shouted the referee. "I've never had a player come apart before."

Meanwhile, my teammates surrounded me and clapped me on the back. The player who tried to tackle me came up, still looking a little stunned, and said, "Here's your leg back." As I sat down to strap it back on, the referee made his final decision.

"It's just as though his jersey had come off," he declared. "Therefore, it's a legal touchdown."

The touchdown made the newspaper the next day and once again I was the center of attention.

There was no doubt in my mind after that—sports was an arena in which I could be an equal.

&

But as I grew into my teenage years, I found that the other kids were getting bigger and stronger than me and competing in sports like basketball and football became more difficult. When I went out for basketball in high school, the team said they wanted me—as a manager. Managers don't play, they pick up balls after practice and make sure the towels are washed and dried. It's an important job, but I always thought of myself as a player and after a couple of months I quit my job as manager and began to look for a sport at which I could compete.

I had to find something I could do that would make me more than just the handicapped kid with the artificial leg. Ironically, soon after that I found just what I had been looking for—something that would change my life forever.

Second Serve

It has been said that a goal is a dream with a deadline. When you set objectives it is important to make them clear and well defined. Dreams are the foundation for our goals, but clarity enables us to hold tenaciously to those goals in times of discouragement and frustration. Vague goals do not provide the inspiration to sustain our motivation. However, ambitious goals not only empower and energize us—they stir our soul and ignite our passion.

Establishing goals that are too easily attained breeds complacency. However, setting goals so far out of reach that we have tremendous difficulty achieving them can be just as deflating. If you are struggling with goal setting, establish a positive structure in your life by writing a list of objectives you will accomplish during the day. Prioritize them in order of importance or enjoyment. As you achieve these tasks you'll feel more capable and self-confident; then you can increase the difficulty and intensity of your goals.

The first thing to remember is to have goals that are uniquely yours (establish goals because they are what you want). Second, be sure you have assessed your talents and abilities; third, visualize yourself accomplishing your goals; and, most important, see yourself as a winner!

Chapter Five

What a Racket!

In 1972 we moved from West Virginia to Danville, California, a city on the east side of the San Francisco Bay. My dad had gotten a job promotion from Kaiser and the relocation came with it. Danville's population was growing like hotcakes when we moved in — there were new cars, new homes, and new shopping malls everywhere you looked. It was a far cry from sleepy little Ravenswood with its one country store and a place at school to keep fishing poles. Most of the kids in Danville wore expensive designer clothes and talked in a lingo I didn't understand — I felt as if we had just moved to a different planet!

I was 12 and once again I was the new kid on the block. It was a lonely time. To get to know somebody I'd have to answer all those questions all over again. And since I was intimidated by these California kids anyway, I kept to myself. It was just my good luck that we moved right across the street from the Greenbrook Racket Club. All I had to do was run down a path, over a little bridge, and I was at the courts. During that first summer in Danville, I got up early every morning and sat on a grassy knoll above the courts and watched the people play.

One day, I was rummaging through our garage and found my Dad's old wooden tennis racket gathering dust on a nail on the wall. I asked him if I could use it and he said yes. The racket was heavy and cumbersome and I had some trouble holding on to it. But I went out and bought some balls and started whacking them against the large green backboard at the end of the courts. I experimented with several methods of holding the racket before I found the best way for me. I held the racket the same way I hold it today—by pinning the grip of the racket to my right elbow with my left hand. However, I couldn't always hold the heavy wooden neck of the racket with my right hand; whenever I would swing hard the racket went flying—which probably accounted for the fact I had very few doubles partners in those days.

It was about that time that Dad and I were browsing through Tony Fisher's sports store. Tony was 29 years old and was the tennis professional at the Greenbrook club. He looked and played a lot like a young version of former tennis great Rod Laver. He was a graduate of San Jose State University and taught science at a local high school. During the summers he played and taught tennis. He was one of the best players in northern California and had the reputation as one of the best tennis instructors in the nation. His mastery of the fundamentals of the game is still next to none.

I used to sit outside the fence when Tony taught

lessons and I'd hang on every word he said. He noticed me after awhile and he would wave and talk to me a little between his lessons. Although I was so bad I couldn't get more than one ball out of ten over the net, he would encourage me and give me small tips. After a few words from Tony, I'd rush down to the backboard and hit balls for hours. But the wooden racket was so heavy I could barely lift it off the ground. Tony used to laugh and say he always knew when I was on the court because he could hear my racket going "scrape," "scrape."

Dad and I were looking at the new rackets in Tony's store because I desperately wanted to find one I could use.

As luck would have it, just before we left I spotted an odd-looking metal racket hanging in the corner. It was a Wilson T-2000 that had two parallel bars connecting the face of the racket to the handle. I picked it up, and my finger accidentally slipped down between the two bars and stuck there. I tried to pull the racket off and it was very snug on my finger. I got excited and shouted, "I can hold onto this racket!" I began to swing it hard and the racket still wouldn't come off. I ran around the store swinging the Wilson T-2000 like a windmill. Customers were ducking for cover and Dad and Tony were cheering and laughing their heads off. But I had finally found what I had been looking for—a racket that would make me a real player.

With my right finger tucked into the neck of the Wilson T-2000, I not only could hold the racket steady, I could serve for the first time because now I could throw the ball up in the air and still grasp the racket. That meant I could play like an able-bodied person. Not only could I serve, I could hit ground strokes and volley. Since I could control the racket better, I became more accurate with my shots. For the first time, I was invited to play doubles.

I practiced every day, mostly against the back-board, and I began to get really excited about tennis. Aside from having to grip the racket in a unique way, I felt I could play because a major part of hitting a tennis ball properly is in turning your shoulders and how you swing the racket with your upper body. I was able to do that easily because my arms and shoulders had become strong, compensating for my lack of fingers. Since I've never been able to grasp anything with my hands, I've had to use my upper body to lift, or hold things. To lift an object, I have to pin it against my chest with my arms, which takes a lot of strength. Also, since I can't grasp things, I have to put my arms all the way under whatever I'm lifting. Con-sequently, my shoulders and upper body had gotten pretty strong and I could put some zip on the ball with a good shoulder turn.

I kept at it and gradually made progress. With my Wilson T-2000, I could hit the ball where I wanted to and my hand–eye coordination kept getting better and better.

By the fall, I began asking some of the other players if I could play with them. One of my favorite playing partners was a young junior player named Carolyn Downing. Carolyn was an excellent player. She also had a model's figure and was very attractive. She was a long-legged blond and she wore short tennis skirts and she beat me like a drum. But I didn't mind.

I also began playing quite a bit with Tony. He would say things like, "Watch the tennis ball until you hear it hit the strings," and other bits of tennis wisdom that I would save like money. To this day, when things go badly for me on the court, I still go back to those basic fundamentals Tony taught me and I usually can straighten out my game.

Looking back, I marvel at how patient Tony was with me. We'd practice for hours, often during the heat of the day when the temperature topped 100 degrees. That was the best time for him because nobody wanted any lessons—it was too hot. I don't know why Tony took me under his wing as he did; plenty of his students had more potential than I did. But Tony liked me. He'd say I was the most "coachable" player he had ever had. Over the next year, our teacher–student relationship blossomed into a friendship and I began going to his house for dinner, where we would spend hours talking about tennis and life in general.

One of the things I appreciated about Tony was the fact he never let up on me. He never treated me like I was handicapped. "Come on, you can do better than that!" he would yell when I missed a shot. Tony would run me from side to side when we played, making me work as hard as he could. Some local players would sometimes chastise Tony for being so tough on me ("Ease up on the handicapped guy"), but Tony never thought of me like that and he never let up. We'd volley at full speed near the net and he'd put me through hours of drills.

Before I discovered the Wilson T-2000, I played in a number of matches—and I lost every one. It was discouraging, though not as bad as it could have been. In a sense, my handicaps took the pressure off me because nobody expected me to win. I was a winner just stepping onto the court. I think being the perpetual underdog allowed me to mentally survive those early defeats. Ironically, had I not been handicapped I might have given up. I was still playing with Dad's old wooden racket and a hard forehand from an opponent would often knock it out of my hands. But I kept playing. Tony once asked me why I kept at it. I told him that being able to play tennis gave me something I could point to and say, "I do that well." It gave me an identity and made me a somebody.

But deep down I wasn't satisfied. I not only wanted to play—I wanted to win.

During one summer, two things happened that turned my game around. First, of course, was the Wilson T-2000 racket. I learned the hard way that I have to tape my finger before a match—or I'd finish the games with a very sore and blistered finger. I hold the grip of the racket to my right elbow with my left hand. I rotate the grip back and forth to hit a forehand, a backhand, and my serve. I can also rotate it to hit a slice, a flat stroke, or a topspin.

The second thing that happened that year was an operation I had on the fingers of my left hand. The operation made my fingers more flexible and allowed me to open them wider. That enabled me for the first time to serve overhand. The surgery included a skin graft from my left thigh and the skin was placed between my two fingers. As a result, I was able to grasp small objects more easily. The surgery was performed at the Shriners Hospital in San Francisco. I saw many small children there, some with artificial legs similar to the ones I wore at their age. It made it easier for me to see these children because I was reminded of the benefits they would gain from surgery.

Prior to the operation it was impossible for me to toss the ball up properly with my left hand so I could serve. Since I can't grasp the ball, I had to learn to balance it on the back of my hand. As I toss the ball up, I squeeze my fingers shut, which propels the ball upward. It literally rolls off the tops of my two fingers. It was a move I couldn't make before I had my hand operation. It's still not an easy move for me to make, and I have to practice it frequently to keep my timing right.

A big problem I had when I was learning tennis and growing up in general, was that when it came to doing physical things, I had no role models! Nobody I knew played tennis like me, so I had to make everything up as I went along. That was particularly difficult in sports, where role models are almost essential. But like most kids, I did adopt a favorite player along the way—Jimmy Connors. I liked Connors for two reasons. First, his tenacity on the court. Jimmy is a fighter and no matter what the situation or score, he never seems to give up. And he wasn't blessed with all the physical skills as were some of the other players of the era, like Bjorn Borg or John McEnroe. But Connors didn't let that stop him from becoming a champion. I felt I could use a little of the Connors' never-say-die attitude.

The second reason I like Connors is that his two-handed backhand is very similar to my two-handed forehand. I carefully studied the way he drew his racket back and I copied his form. It's worked for me. When I was 14, Tony gave me a huge poster of Connors and it hung in my room for several years as a reminder of the quality of tennis I wanted to achieve.

Once I discovered the Wilson T-2000 racket, I became obsessed with tennis. I played all day long on weekends and after school during the week. At first, it wasn't the winning that sustained my interest, it was simply the fact that I could compete against able-bodied players. That gave me a sense that I belonged. My tennis skills became a kind of emotional pillar that could hold me up whenever things went badly— and they frequently did. The hardest thing for me to deal with during my teenage years was the harassment I got from the other kids. The younger children I could usually handle without much problem. They'd yell something derogatory about my hands and I would walk over to them and look them right in the eye.

As a way to mask my insecurities, I became the butt of my own jokes. "Don't *you* ever play with firecrackers," I'd say to them in a solemn voice. Sometimes I'd tell them I was a surfer and was attacked by sharks. Having my hands mutilated by firecrackers or sharks was very impressive to the younger kids and they'd leave me alone. But the older kids, especially the young teenagers who hung around the tennis courts, could be merciless. Most of the time the boys liked to tease me when there were girls around so they looked like big shots. I usually laughed off their jokes — I never let them see me get upset — but afterwards I'd go home and cry.

I wasn't aware of how badly that teasing hurt me until just a couple of years ago when I gave a presentation to an insurance underwriters group near San Francisco. A man came up to me after the presentation and slapped me on the back like we were old buddies. I recognized him as one of the boys who used to taunt me and I suddenly got very angry. I didn't hit him, which is what I felt like doing, but I made it clear we weren't buddies either. When I had a chance to think about it later, I was surprised at how much resentment I still felt, deep down. I thought I had exorcised most of my bitterness, but I was wrong. I guess some scars require a lifetime of healing.

I practically lived on the courts and under Tony's watchful eye, I improved quickly. It wasn't long before I was doing more than just competing — I began to win.

But there was something else that attracted me to tennis. In talking to athletes from all different sports I've found that there is a common, hard-to-describe experience that happens once in a while during the execution of physical exercise. Runners call it "getting a second wind," basketball players refer to it as "shooting the lights out," and in tennis we call it "hitting the zone." It's a time when body, soul, and mind all come together in perfect sync and it's the best, most natural high there is. It's a feeling you can't really play for, it just has to happen. Everything seems to flow and time really stops being relevant. During those matches when I hit the zone, I feel completely free to do or be anything I want to be. I can transcend, even if only for the moment, the earthbound realities of my hands and leg—I'm an equal among equals. Competition, pressure, intensity, and long and hard practice sessions are all ingredients to being able to play in the zone, but the rest of the ingredients are intangibles. It usually occurs during a good competitive match. And a funny thing happens when I hit the zone—I can play for hours without really remembering the match. I remember the score goes well, but I'm not really conscious of any peripheral objects or events. To me, "zoning" is one of the wonderful and unexpected gifts I've gotten from tennis and one of the great joys of my life.

꒰꒱

In tennis, as in life, you never really "make it." There isn't an end to the road, only the journey. We may win or lose a big match, but there always comes another one. Even Bjorn Borg, as great as he was, was only champion until his next match. But then, the real joy is in the playing.

Chapter Six

Making the Team

By the time I entered Monte Vista High School, California and I had finally gotten used to each other. The school was full of bright, energetic kids, many of whom would go on to successful careers. These were the kids of high-achieving parents, who grew up with the expectations to excel. That feeling of confidence had spilled over from the classrooms onto the athletic fields. No wonder the Monte Vista tennis team was consistently one of the top teams in the country.

As a freshman and a newcomer, I was ignorant of all that, which was just as well: I didn't know enough to be intimidated. All I knew was that I couldn't wait for tennis season.

It came sooner than I expected. I had been in school for about two weeks when I spotted a notice that all players interested in trying out for the varsity tennis team should report to the tennis courts after school. I started to get really nervous, even though I had been playing tennis all summer. I didn't have my tennis gear with me so I borrowed a dime and called Mom. I used the only phone available, which was in a quiet study hall, full of students. You could hear a pin drop in the hall, so when I spoke on the phone, it was like announcing my conversation over a loud-speaker.

Mom answered.

"Mom, I need you to bring my tennis racket, my tennis clothes, and my running leg."

Steven Spielberg couldn't have directed it better—all the heads in the study hall raised up in unison and stared at me. I managed a weak little smile and shrugged.

I should explain that I have both a walking leg and a running leg. The foot on my running leg is much more flexible than the one on my walking leg. It also has a rubber insert that slips over my leg, which makes it more secure. Although it's more flexible, I can't wear it as long as I can my walking leg.

I was bouncing off the wall all afternoon. I don't think I absorbed much history or math that day. It was embarrassing that Mom had to bring my gear, so I arranged to meet her at a church just up the street from the school. I was mortified to see that she brought my gear in a paper sack! All the other kids had designer tennis bags and here I was, with my jock strap, my leg, and all the rest of my stuff in a paper sack.

I managed to sneak into the back of the locker room without being seen and slipped on my gear and my running leg and hustled out to the courts. The first person I met was our coach, Floyd Baker. Coach Baker is tall, silver-haired and a former pro baseball player. He's one of the finest people I've ever had the pleasure of knowing. He always encouraged us and he had the uncanny ability to make everybody on the team feel important. Whether you were the best player or the worst, he treated you the same. On most squads, only the top players got uniforms — Coach Baker made sure that everybody on our team received one. He also took everybody to away matches, whether or not they were going to play. He spent an equal amount of time with each player and in doing so he made everyone feel important. To me, he still epitomizes the ideal high school coach — someone who is as interested in helping a child grow and gain self-confidence as he is in winning.

Until that day, Coach Baker knew nothing about me. I often wonder what he must have thought when he saw me. But Coach Baker never let on. He walked right up to me and shook my hand. I was thrilled. Yet, Coach Baker did it like it was the most natural thing in the world. I was so excited and warmed by that gesture that I felt my feet were floating about six inches above the courts.

He introduced all the players, then told us to warm up for the challenge matches. He wrote our names on a piece of paper, then matched us up at random. As luck would have it, I was matched up against one of the best players on the team, John Balmer. John was a senior and had played on the varsity singles squad the year before. We were assigned to the front court.

We started warming up and I felt good. I was striking the ball crisply and placing it right where I wanted it. I think John was a little shocked when I sizzled a few practice shots his way.

When the match started, I hit my stride right away. I was doing everything well and John Balmer was perhaps the most surprised kid in northern California. He immediately got frustrated with himself. It was a difficult situation for him. I'm sure he wasn't prepared mentally for a tough match. We played three sets. I won the first and he the second. By the end of the second set, all the other matches had been completed, so the entire tennis team was on the sideline, watching us battle it out. Everybody was cheering for me. It was more than John could take and I won the third set going away. The team erupted into cheers and everybody spilled out onto the court to shake my hand and congratulate me. I was overwhelmed. I hadn't had so many people shake my hand in my entire life! Everybody wanted to know how I held the racket and how my leg worked. I was accepted by the team from that day on and in time even John Balmer began to appreciate what a great day it had been for me. After the commotion died down and everybody went to shower, I raced up to the study hall and called Dad at work. "Old Mr. Tough Guy" got choked up and couldn't talk for a moment after I told him about the match.

The win did wonders for my confidence. The news spread throughout the school and kids were coming up to me and introducing themselves — I was on Cloud Nine.

But I still had a long way to go to become an accomplished tennis player. I was running and reacting better on the court, but my serve was weak and I didn't volley that well. I was still in touch with Tony, though, and he was a constant source of advice and encouragement. He'd say, "All you need to do is hit the ball over the net one more time than the other guy." He taught me consistency—a trait that is vastly overlooked in sports and in life. Ultimately, it isn't the clever shot that makes the pro. It is being able to get up every day and rise to a certain level of excellence, regardless of the circumstances.

My tennis game is built on that one fundamental—consistency. Get the ball over the net one more time than the other guy and wait for him to make a mistake. I'm not overpowering, I just keep the ball deep and try to pin my opponent down on the base line. Tony taught me to stay within myself when I play, to do what I do best. He would say, "Focus in on your strengths, don't try to do something that's not natural. Don't neglect your weaknesses, but in a match, focus on your strengths."

Because of all the encouragement, I was playing with growing confidence and I made the varsity team as the number four player (out of five singles players). That first year, Monte Vista won 14 matches and lost 2. My personal record was 11 wins and 3 losses.

During my sophomore year, our team started one of the greatest winning streaks ever recorded by a large high school in California. The team was loaded with talent. Three of our top players went on to play on the professional tour, including Tripp Gordon, Doug Stone, and Jeff Southwick, whose serve was once the fastest ever clocked in the world. Playing with those guys and for Coach Baker was a tremendous thrill for me. *We didn't lose a single match for the next three years.*

We won 46 matches in a row and three consecutive East Bay Athletic League titles. By my senior year, our winning streak had generated national attention and Monte Vista was considered the top prep team in the country. My personal record during my four years at Monte Vista was 47 wins and 6 losses—half my losses came in my freshman year.

દ્ર

But it wasn't always smooth going. Whenever we would play an away game with a school we hadn't played before, people rooting for the other team would spot my artificial leg and the hoots and catcalls would start from the bleachers. I'd like to say that I got used to them, but I never did and often—although I was careful never to show it on the court—the heckling would really get me down. While I was on the court, however, I learned to use anger as motivation.

When I was 16—during the summer between my junior and senior year at Monte Vista—I played in a junior tournament and was matched against one of the top ranked junior players in northern California. This player (I'll call him Al) was a good-looking kid. He had fancy clothes and three or four tennis rackets and a brand new car in the parking lot. By this time, I had replaced my old paper sack with a decent tennis bag, but I was still feeling intimidated by this hot-shot.

Tony was there to watch the match and as I walked by him, he leaned forward and told me that no matter how many rackets Al had on the bench, the rules said he could only use one on the court. Of course, it was Tony's way of telling me not to get psyched out by Al's reputation.

As we took the court, Al's friends in the stands saw me and began to laugh. They were laughing at me and I knew it. Al heard them and he began to mock me as we warmed up. He would run with an exaggerated limp and serve with two hands. At first, I felt sick and wanted to run off and hide. But then, I just got mad. Al and his friends were going to be in for a long day, if I had anything to do with it. At the same time, Al was getting lackadaisical and seemed to be more interested in entertaining his friends than in preparing to play me.

I was hot and started off fast—I passed him with ease and my serves were quick and accurate. Al was mighty surprised that I was giving him a fight, and started to berate himself verbally. Before long he was punching the air in frustration and he began looking at his strings as if there was something wrong with his racket. His friends began yelling, "Come on, Al, you can beat this guy!"

"Shut up!" Al screamed back at them.

I looked over at Tony and he grinned. Without saying anything, I knew what Tony was thinking. He detested showoffs and he was delighted to see me stick it to this kid.

Al reacted in desperation. He began drop-shotting me—hitting short shots up by the net—in order to make me run. His strategy was to make me run to the net to get the drop-shot, then try to lob my return back over my head. Like a lot of guys, he thought because of my leg I wouldn't be able to run well. While I'm not the fastest guy in the world, I can get around the court quicker than most people think and I was holding my own against Al's drop-shot strategy.

I was slightly ahead in the match when Al mis-hit a lob and it was coming down short, right where I could smash it. I jumped up to get better leverage and came down on my left leg—and it completely snapped in half! My foot went skidding across the court and hit the fence and there was an explosion of sawdust from my ruined leg. I fell flat on my back. From my vantage point, I could just see Tony on the sideline, laughing his head off. Everybody else in the stands was aghast and Al's eyes were as big as saucers. He jumped over the net and knelt down to see if I was okay. Poor Al, he wasn't sure what had happened—he thought he had crippled me. Meanwhile, Tony, who was still laughing, ran up the hill to my car and got my backup leg. (I always bring two to matches—just in case.)

By the time I put my new leg on, Al was totally psyched out. His friends were still standing courtside with their mouths hanging open. I breezed through the third set and won the match. Afterwards, a photographer took our picture, a copy of which my parents still have in their scrapbook. It shows Al decked out in his designer clothes, holding his three rackets under his arm. He's also holding a tiny trophy and on his face is the biggest frown you've ever seen in your life. I'm standing next to him and I've got a huge trophy and a smile to match.

During my junior year I was playing a tough match against a good player from California High School in San Ramon. My opponent was on his game that day and, for some reason, I was having trouble getting focused. We had split the first two sets, but in the third and deciding set, he was beating me handily. I was down five games to none. If I lost one more game, the match was history.

The other matches were over and the players were crowded around the outside fence. My team-mates started cheering me on to make a comeback. I started thinking about advice Tony had given me. "Forget about the score and play one point at a time. Concentrate and block everything else out of your mind." Suddenly, I started playing with more con-fidence. I started hitting the corners and driving my opponent from baseline to baseline. I won my ser-vice, then broke his. I could feel the momentum switching to my side and I started playing with con-fidence. I rallied to win seven straight games to win the match and keep our streak alive.

The local media made a big deal out of my come-back and the television station KTVU in Oakland decided to feature my next match on the local news. The following week the TV crews set up shop around Monte Vista and I was center of attention — a king for a day.

But when the match started, the king fell off his throne with a resounding thud.

All the attention I was receiving for my tennis was a new phenomenon for me. For most of my school years prior to high school, I hadn't quite fit in, and was almost a novelty to the other kids. I made up for all those frustrations by enjoying this attention as much as I could. I hammed it up around my friends and became the class clown. My grades slipped, but

I didn't care. In a way I became addicted to the attention my classmates and the community were lavishing on me—the more I got, the more I wanted.

But like any addict, I paid the price for my addiction. The word got around that KTVU was going to film my match and the school was abuzz with the news. Pretty soon I thought I was a mix of Tom Selleck and Bjorn Borg, but I learned the hard way otherwise.

The match was against Amador Valley High School in Pleasanton, a suburban city in the East Bay area. Usually, only a couple dozen people would watch our matches, but the television coverage made it an event and that afternoon the stands were packed with students.

The camera crew filmed me taping my finger and getting ready for the match. I noticed the size of the crowd and suddenly I began to get nervous. Like a dark cloud, doubts began entering my mind. What would happen if I lost? What would I do? How would I act? I began visualizing walking to the net after the match and making up an excuse as to why I lost. I was visualizing defeat and sure enough, when the match began, I got what players call a "cement elbow." It felt like my arm weighed 500 pounds. I wasn't hitting any of my normal shots and I was blowing easy ones. I kept smiling for the camera, but Roger Crawford, movie star, was about to become Roger Crawford, the has-been.

For the first time since I took up tennis, I started getting mad at myself. I stopped playing to win and started playing not to lose. My opponent sensed my confusion and he moved in for the kill. He whipped me in two sets in front of my first regional television audience. I was humiliated, but in time I realized that match had taught me some valuable lessons.

First, I learned that without a clear focus on the job at hand, that job won't get done properly. Second, I realized you can't rest on your laurels. If you do, somebody is sure to yank them out from under you. Finally, it taught me just how powerful expectations can be. Once I visualized how I was going to act after losing, there was no doubt I was going to lose. A negative outlook nearly always becomes a self-fulfilling prophecy. The problem is, while a positive attitude takes a lot of hard work to build and constant vigilance to maintain, a negative attitude can sneak up on you when you're not looking and if you don't watch out—whap!—it lowers the boom.

I believe that, often, people fail to achieve because of two extreme attitudes. Either they set expectations at an unrealistic level, or they don't have any expectations at all. To be successful, to develop growing confidence, you have to set realistic goals, then take pleasure in their achievement. Confidence comes from knowing you are good at what you do.

When I was a junior at Monte Vista, I was voted captain of the tennis team. It meant a lot to me to have the younger players looking up to me for guidance. Me! Old lobster hands! I remember wishing that the doctors who told my parents that I would never be able to care for myself could see me now. I'd tell them, "Hi guys, care to play a set or two?" Then I'd beat their pants off.

As it turned out, being captain of the team was good experience for my speaking career. The team would always ask me to give them pep talks before the matches and I could get everybody all fired up. I didn't know then that I was honing the skills for my life's work.

Monte Vista held a sports banquet at the end of every year and there was one that I'll never forget. After all the regular athletic awards were handed out, Coach Baker got up and addressed the audience. He told them a new annual award had been created for the athlete who best demonstrated exceptional drive, inspiration, and leadership.

Coach Baker said, "We will always remember that the player for whom the award is named showed us what personal power you can have through motivation and through a dream. Because this unusual tennis player showed us that dreams really do come true. This is the Roger Crawford Award."

At the end of his speech, Coach Baker started crying and the place fell apart. Even the big tough football players cried like babies. Everybody gave me big hugs — I was squashed by the time the football team finished hugging me.

During my junior year, I was lucky enough to be named athlete of the week for our school and was therefore invited to the prestigious Northern California Athlete of the Year Award Ceremony. The banquet and ceremony was held in the Flecto Center in Oakland. Former Los Angeles Raider quarterback Ken Stabler was the keynote speaker and a number of players from the San Francisco 49ers and Raider teams were there. The event was always well covered by the media statewide, so there were reporters and television cameras everywhere. I was awed by the whole thing and I sat throughout most of the ceremonies looking for celebrities and pointing them out to my parents. I was having a great time, but I wasn't paying much attention to the ceremonies themselves.

Finally, it became time to introduce the Male Athlete of the Year. Gene Upshaw, former Raider great, was to present the award and he began speaking. He read the record of the winner's achievements and he was talking about this and that and I wasn't really listening to him. I was busy talking to the people around me and to my parents. Finally, he said, "And he happens to wear an artificial leg."

That got my attention. "Wow," I said to Dad, "That's great. Somebody won who has a leg like mine!" It really made me feel good to know there was somebody else like me who had succeeded in sports. So I started looking around for the one-legged guy who was going to get the award. And then Upshaw said, "And he has a deformity of both hands." Then it dawned on me—I had won!

There were 2,000 people in the center and they all erupted in cheers and applause. I barely remember walking up to get the award, but I do remember shaking Gene Upshaw's huge paw and thanking my coaches and my mom and dad for all they had done. It was quite a moment.

In my last high school match, I played a freshman from a nearby high school and I beat him pretty easily. After the match, I was putting my stuff away in my tennis bag and this timid little freshman approached me and thrust out his hand. "Mr. Crawford," he said. "It's been an honor to play you." I just stared at him for a moment. It occurred to me, as I shook the boy's hand, that I had just come full circle.

Second Serve

Perseverance comes from the love of what we want to achieve, and an unwavering confidence that tells us we can do it. It is fortified by the belief that our goals in life are valuable, exciting, and worthy of our best effort. In order to utilize our perseverance, we must first have a clear vision of what we want to accomplish, and then accept the inevitable roadblocks along the way.

No one can gain perseverance overnight; it is developed gradually. But we can begin by making a short-term commitment. This will give us valuable experience that will help us establish more long-term commitments. Perseverance is the secret to effective living. It involves applying the discipline to remain consistent, regardless of the obstacles or the odds. Without perseverance there is no achievement—and no success.

Chapter Seven

Fitting In

While my high school tennis career had turned out better than I ever could have hoped, I still struggled to fit in socially with the other students at Monte Vista. At first, I was very shy and it took me a long time to make friends. The early teenage years can be tough for any kid, but if you happen to be different, you're usually left out. Regardless of how much I wanted to fit in with my classmates, no matter what clothes I wore, or how I cut my hair, I was always going to be different.

I had gone to junior high school in Danville and although I didn't make any close friendships, I had gotten to know most of the kids in my class and at least they knew about my hands and leg. I was comfortable being around most of them and I was looking forward to joining them in our first year of high school.

But the school board had different ideas. A couple of months before I was to enter high school, the board changed the school boundaries slightly, just enough to bump me into another high school district. Instead of going to San Ramon High School with all my friends, I suddenly had to go to Monte Vista, which was at the opposite end of town. Once again I had to start all over again making new friends.

During the first week at Monte Vista, I walked around the school with my hands in my pockets, wishing I was invisible. As usual, I had to deal with the startled looks of the students when they got a good look at my hands and I had to answer all the questions all over again. I was miserable. The worst part of all was walking past the Senior Bench. Upperclassmen were always loafing around a large wooden bench located in the courtyard under a covered walkway. The Senior Bench was a launching pad for salvos of insults that rained down on any underclass students who happened to walk past. They'd whistle at the girls and make fun of the boys. Like most of the other freshmen, I avoided the Senior Bench at all costs.

During the first month of school, I began to have trouble with one particular senior, who took it upon himself to heckle me whenever he could. He had the personality of a weasel and a mouth that wouldn't quit. His taunting got so bad that I dreaded going to school in the morning. He liked to sit around on the Senior Bench, which is one reason I always tried to avoid it.

One day it was pouring rain and, to keep from getting wet, I decided to try and sneak past the Senior Bench. Of course, my nemesis was there and he immediately got all over me. I was so mad I felt like dropping my books and taking a swing at him, but my hands aren't built for fighting and besides, he was a lot bigger than I was. He was really giving it to me when around the corner came big Casey Merrill. Casey was a senior and a football star. He went on to play professional football for the Cleveland Browns and the Green Bay Packers, as a defensive end. Even in high school, Casey Merrill was a very large person, about 6'4" and 240 pounds. He always wore flannel shirts rolled up over his huge biceps. Casey was one of the nicest guys in school, but nobody messed with him, either.

Casey and I knew each other slightly because football and tennis were both played in the fall and we saw each other in the locker room after practice. Casey had heard what was going on before he came around the corner and he strode over to the boy who was giving me trouble. He grabbed him by the throat and lifted him a foot off the ground and slammed him against the flag pole.

"If you say one more thing to that kid, I'm going to bite your head off," growled Casey.

The kid turned an interesting purple color and coughed out a promise never to taunt me again.

The word got around pretty fast that Casey Merrill had taken me under his wing and I enjoyed a heckle-free year after that. Casey remained a source of strength for me because he encouraged me at every turn and he inspired other people to encourage me, too.

৵

During my freshman year I met Ron Piombo and Ray Hunt, who became my ace pals. Ron was an inch over six feet tall and was built like a blacksmith.

He was Italian, had jet-black hair and loved a good time. He was an oversized Donny Ponzoni.

Ray was a good-looking Irish lad with sandy brown hair and a medium build. He was the Dapper Dan of our trio — he wore starched shirts and slacks when the rest of us came to school in t-shirts and blue jeans.

Our lockers were near each other and it was inevitable that we would see each other often. What I liked most about the two of them was how straightforward they were. Although I hadn't really shaken hands with anybody except my parents and the guys on the tennis team, the very first day I met Ray and Ron, they both stuck out their hands.

We became fast friends and they remain my closest friends to this day. They were the first friends I ever had that I could talk to about things other than my handicaps — having friends like that was new for me. We talked for hours about our futures: the type of jobs we wanted and the kinds of cars we'd have and the type of women we wanted to marry. Their friendship meant a great deal to me because they both accepted me as a peer. In all the time we were together in high school, we never talked about my handicaps. In fact, sometimes they forgot all about them, which was one of the greatest compliments they could have given me. Once Ron asked me what type of class ring I was going to buy and I had to remind him that I can't wear rings. "Oh yeah," he said and we both laughed.

As a freshman, I had not yet learned to tie my shoes. One day one came untied. Ron spotted my dangling lace and in the middle of the crowded hall he stopped and asked if he could tie it for me. I don't think Ron gave it a second thought, but I'll never forget it—to me it was a real act of friendship.

Ron, Ray and Roger—we were known as the Three Roosters—we were inseparable.

Fitting in with the rest of the freshman class wasn't as easy, though. Most of the kids still stared at me and I'm sure many of them assumed that I was mentally handicapped, as well. I sought to overcome that obstacle by becoming what I had been in elementary school—the class clown.

One practical joke, in particular, made Ray and me notorious. One day we had a substitute teacher in English, a very prim and proper lady whose demeanor was a little on the stilted side. She was the perfect foil for a practical joke.

All the kids were in the English room, but class had not started yet. Ray and I staged a terrible fight that we had choreographed beforehand. The rest of the kids weren't sure if the fight was for real, so they were all watching to see what was going to happen. Before the teacher could react to break us up, Ray knocked me down and grabbed my artificial foot. We had already undone the bolt that kept my foot rigid to my leg, so when he twisted my foot, it spun around like crazy. The substitute teacher was horrified. She screamed at Ray to stop, she was sure my foot was broken. The kids roared with laughter. The teacher caught on after I started laughing. Luckily for us she turned out to be a pretty good sport. She forced a smile and told us to go sit down. To this day, when we get together, my old classmates still talk about the time Ray spun my foot around in English class.

The streaking craze was then in vogue. Taking your clothes off and running as fast as you could through a crowded area was all the rage. Even the Academy Award ceremony for the motion picture industry was streaked the year I was a junior. Late in the year, about ten guys in our class decided to streak the front lawn area where the kids usually caught the school bus. I didn't think of myself as especially good streaking material, but I wanted to fit in, so I agreed to go with them. We took off all our clothes except our tennis shoes, and we put ski masks over our faces. I had such a positive attitude that I wore a ski mask, too.

As we streaked by, we could hear the kids shouting, "Who's that? Who's that? Hey, there's Roger! Hey, Roger, what're you doing?"

At a school assembly later in the year, the students gave me a plaque for being the "Biggest Exhibitionist." I was really embarrassed by the whole thing, but in a way I thought it was a compliment, too. It was certainly better than being named the "Tiniest Exhibitionist."

But if humor helped me fit in, it also got me in trouble once in a while. When I first started making friends in high school, I used to pal around with a group of kids. One of our Friday night entertainments was to go to the swanky Round Hill Country Club with big blocks of ice. We would sneak out onto the golf course, haul the ice blocks to the top of some big hills, then sit on them and slide down. You could fly down the hill on those blocks of ice and we thought it was great fun. But I guess the golfers weren't too amused to find streak marks on the fairway the next morning, and one Friday night the police dropped a dragnet around us. Most of the kids were on top of the hill when they saw the police cars drive up and they managed to scatter and get away. But not me. By the time I saw what was happening, I was halfway down the hill, sliding as fast as I could on a block of ice right toward the long arm of the law. Two of Danville's finest caught me when I reached the bottom and marched me back to the police car.

"You're in big trouble, son," one of them said.

I was trembling.

"Put out your hands." He was going to handcuff me. Later, I realized he was just doing that to scare us and keep us off the golf course, but at that point I thought I was going to be taken away to jail. He slapped the cuffs on my left hand, but when he put the other cuff on my right hand, it fell right off! The policeman looked at the cuffs dangling off my left wrist and broke up laughing. "I've never, ever, seen anybody slip through a handcuff before," he said, and he called the other cops over to have a look. After marveling over how I could get out of the handcuffs, they drove me down to the golf clubhouse and called my parents. My parents were not amused, even when they heard the story about the handcuffs, and I was grounded for a month.

Fitting in at high school isn't easy if you can't eat fast food. With my hands being the way they are, it is almost impossible for me to hold some foods. I can still recall the first meal I ever ate in the cafeteria at Monte Vista. As I was standing in line, I looked up at the menu on the wall. The two main items on the menu were tacos and burritos. I felt sick—there are not two more difficult foods for me to eat in the whole world. But Mom had purchased me a lunch ticket, so I was stuck. It was either don't eat, or try to wrestle with the tacos. To make matters worse, the tacos they served at my high school were the exploding type. You take one bite and they explode all over the place.

I considered not eating, but my empty stomach convinced me that hunger was not the better part of valor, so I gave the first taco a try. I took a bite and shredded cheese, tomatoes, onions, and taco meat exploded in all directions. To make matters worse, I dropped the rest of it on the floor. I looked up and there must have been 20 kids staring at me. I was terribly embarrassed. I wanted to find a giant hole and crawl into it. But there was no hole big enough and I had no choice but to keep eating. I broke up the second taco and ate it, piece by piece, knowing that half the people in the lunch room were watching me eat.

Another big problem was typing class. About two weeks before school started I got my class schedule and there it was, right behind world history—TYPING I. It may as well have read AGONY I. For the next two weeks, that's all I could think about; me trying to type. Typing noises haunted me everywhere I went, I even dreamed about typing. By the time school started and I reluctantly entered my second-hour typing class, I was a wreck. I was already self-conscious because I was the new kid and now I had to type in front of everybody! With only a big thumb on one hand and a thumb and a finger on the other hand, how was I going to type? It may as well have been a class on learning to eat with chopsticks. There was just no way.

Thankfully, the typing teacher saw my dilemma right away and he made allowances for me, although I think it totally screwed up his teaching style. He was so conscious not to offend me that he'd say, "Everybody hold your hands like this — uh, except for you, Roger. You just do it any way you can." It was nice of him to interrupt the class to give me special instructions, but it was hopeless. Every time I tried to type I would hit two keys with my right thumb because it is so large. I was the only person in class who typed with a stutter! It was very frustrating for me and the guys around me couldn't help but laugh every time I hit two keys at once. I was such a disturbance that I was finally excused. I learned a good lesson, though. You can't do *everything* — it's better to concentrate on what you *can* do.

Teaching is one of the most underrated professions. Teachers have one of the most important jobs in the world, and the best ones can make a marked difference in a child's life. I know they did in mine.

One of those special teachers was my psychology instructor, Julie MacMillan, or "Mrs. Mac," as we called her. She was a positive, upbeat person. A couple of times during the year, she would have us do an exercise called the "hot seat." She had the entire class sit in a circle with one student in the middle. Then she would have each student in the circle say something positive about the person sitting in the middle. In the beginning, the class was uncomfortable with this because in high school it's not "cool" to say nice things to each other. What the "hot seat" did was make it okay for us to compliment each other because the teacher was making us do it.

I was very nervous when it came to my turn to be in the middle of the group. I prepared myself for the worst. I was in for a surprise. They used words like, "strong," "courageous," and "confident." One girl even said "cute." I began to look around to see if someone else was sitting in the circle with me! These kids had a lot better image of me than I had of myself. I often wonder whether corporations wouldn't do well to have their employees sit on the "hot seat." A positive stroke now and then can do wonders for employee morale.

Later that year, Mrs. Mac gave us an assignment to bring our baby pictures to class, then write a short history of our life. I had rarely seen pictures of myself when I was a tot and I was very nervous. I always wondered how my parents reacted to me when I was an infant.

My mom rustled around in the closet for awhile, then brought out a box of old photographs. One showed my aunts holding up their babies to the camera — and there was my mom, holding me right along with the others. It meant a lot. My parents could have easily hidden me away at that age and I never would have known it. That was wonderful for me because I had always thought that my parents would frown in their pictures with me. After all, wouldn't they be unhappy or embarrassed having a handicapped child? As you can see, against all the evidence, I was having a hard time accepting their full acceptance of me.

For my school assignment, I chose a picture that showed my father and me and four other fathers and their sons at Disneyland. All of us had on Mickey Mouse hats and each father was holding his son's hand. There was my Dad, with his Mickey Mouse hat on, holding my hand, smiling hugely for the camera.

ॐ

In time, I began to feel more comfortable at Monte Vista. The kids began to know me more as a tennis player and a person and less as "the handicapped guy." I was fitting in.

But I'll never forget Prom Night of my junior year. That was the time I found out the hard way that my success in fitting in didn't apply to tuxedos.

Ray, Ronnie, and I all had dates, and a few days before the prom we drove down to the rental outlet together to pick out our tuxedos. As you can imagine, I'm not an off-the-rack kind of guy. My coat size is a 42-short-short-short.

When we got there, Ronnie picked out a size 44 coat that fit him perfectly. Ray picked a size 40 that fit beautifully. Then the poor salesman came to me and said, "What size do you wear?" I told him a size 42. He brought me a jacket, which fit just right around the shoulders, but the arms just about hit the floor. The salesman looked at me and said, "It looks like we're going to have to do a little alteration."

He promised he would have the coat adjusted by the night of the dance. I didn't think anything more about it until about two hours before the prom, when it was time to go back to the place to pick up our coats. I found my coat and pants were altered perfectly, but there was still a problem with the shirt. Because of my short arms, the shirt sleeves were about a foot too long!

"No problem," the salesman said. "We'll just fold back the sleeves," and he shoved the sleeves back under my coat. I was pleased; his trick seemed to work.

My date for the prom was a very pretty and popular young lady named Kerry Robinson. I remembered to pull my hands out of my pockets and put a smile on my face when I asked her, and I was ecstatic when she said yes.

I got to drive Dad's car to the dance and I had spent all day polishing it so it gleamed even in the moonlight. I put on my tux, folded my shirt sleeves back, and drove over to Kerry's house. Her father met me at the door.

"Mr. Robinson, it's very nice to see you," I said and thrust my hand out. Immediately, my shirt sleeve came unfolded and shot out of my coat sleeve like a fake snake from a trick can. He stood there speech-less, searching for my hand while I groped around, trying to pull in my sleeve. I was terribly embarrassed, but he just smiled and asked me inside. I was still flustered when I got inside and met Mrs. Robinson. She was all smiles and asked me to sit down. As we waited for Kerry, Mrs. Robinson made small talk and asked me what I wanted to do with my life. I was very nervous, which, as usual, meant I was about to tell a bad joke. All I could think of at the time was a private joke my dad and I had together. He told me that if I wanted to get a laugh when anybody asked me what I wanted to be when I grew up, I should say I wanted to be a brain surgeon. So that's what I said.

"Mrs. Robinson, I'd like to be a brain surgeon."

The poor Robinsons looked at me with little patronizing smiles and just nodded. They didn't want to laugh for fear I was being serious and it would hurt my feelings. The only feeling I had at the time was that prom night wasn't starting out very well.

The rest of the night was better, though, and Kerry and I had a wonderful time. We danced all evening. But of all the things that happened on prom night, I'll always remember poor old Mr. Robinson searching for my hand in miles of shirt sleeve.

I received an unexpected surprise my senior year. I was selected Homecoming King by the student body. It was a big moment. Was it a sympathy vote? Perhaps for some, but not for most. I am very aware that having a physical handicap can invoke sympathy. That's not necessarily a bad thing, it's how you deal with that sympathy that counts — because for the physically handicapped that sympathy can be a double-edged sword.

Why?

Because once you start believing in that sympathy, it gives you a wonderful excuse to fail. There are people who, if accommodated by their peers, will find a liability in their life and then blame every failure on their so-called disability. That's why having a visible physical handicap can let you off the hook every single time. I could point to my hands and my leg every time I failed — or every time I didn't try — as an excuse, and most people would buy it. Sympathy, even when given in the spirit of kindness and friendship, can be a seductive and dangerous thing.

Another seduction is not to fall prey to what I call the "what if" syndrome. There are a lot of people who spend their entire lives saying and dreaming about "what if" this, or "what if" that. What would have happened if I had been born with ten fingers, or what if I had two normal legs, or what if society had treated me better. The "what if" syndrome is a dead-end street. I try to think in terms of what is, rather than what if.

ॐ

In my travels, people often ask me if there was an operation to provide me with normal hands and legs, would I undergo it.

My answer is no.

Fifteen years ago, my answer would have been different. But today, in all honesty, my answer would be no. I realize now that it was my physical handicap that caused me to focus in on my strengths and deal with my limitations a lot earlier than I would have if I had been able-bodied. For example, I wondered, will somebody love me? What will I do for a living? What will my career be? I was forced to think about those things very early. My handicap also forced me to deal with rejection very early. Everybody has to do that sooner or later; I had to do it sooner. Developing the strength to say, "I'm okay," is perhaps the single most important lesson that anyone can learn. As you can see from my continual striving for acceptance, it is still a battle for me. But not in a fundamental way, as it once was. Down deep I now know who I am.

Chapter Eight

My First Dance

Most of my classmates began dating during freshman year. Dating meant going out to the movies, dancing, and holding hands. My lifelong fear that no one would ever want to hold my hand was never far from the surface and I decided to forget about girls and focus my energy on tennis.

However, in spite of my intentions, girls were very much on my mind. I hadn't forgotten the square dance fiasco when my classmate reacted in horror at the prospect of touching my hands. Most teenage boys go through an insecure stage with girls, but for me that insecurity took on epic proportions. Eventually, my fears got the worst of me and I began to suffer severe stomach problems and had to see a doctor.

But my parents, especially Mom, encouraged me to go to the school dances and my resolve slowly crumbled. In the fall of my freshman year, I decided it was time to give dating a try. There was a freshman dance and I got all dressed up in my leisure suit, my angel flight pants, and my puka shell necklace, and I even slicked my hair back. I was all ready to go, my parents were heading out the door to drive me to school, when I chickened out. I just couldn't do it. I told my parents that I didn't have a date and all my other friends did — I just wouldn't feel right being the only guy going alone. I gave in to my apprehensions, beat a hasty retreat to my bedroom, and fell into a deep gloom.

The following Monday I had a nice surprise. A lot of girls asked me where I had been during the dance. I was shocked! They had missed me! The air started coming back into my chest and I began to feel a lot better.

But dancing still worried me. Especially slow dancing. During the slow dances, of course, you had to hold hands and I felt that no girl would want to hold my hand. I decided that when the band played a slow dance, I was going to make for the only safe place around — the boys' bathroom. That thought gave me some solace.

By Christmas, I had worked up my nerve enough to take another crack at this dancing business. The school was hosting the Winter Carnival Dance in the gymnasium and I was determined to go. I got all dressed up again and this time I actually went through with it. I went stag and my parents dropped me off at the door.

The night started out great. I walked in and was greeted by a number of kids. I began to relax and as the band set up, we all drank punch and talked and I gained confidence. I was feeling good when the band began to play and people started to dance. I decided it was now or never. I put my punch glass down and walked up to a group of girls. Halfway there, though, I began to lose my nerve. I walked with my head down and my hands went into my pockets.

"I don't suppose you want to dance," was my suave approach.

The girl smiled, but shook her head no.

I had expected her reaction and I made straight for the boys' room. I hung around for awhile and washed my hands about 30 times. Then I realized that none of the other girls had laughed at me when I was turned down. I decided to try again.

I walked over to a group of girls, but again I lost my confidence and approached them with my head down and my hands in my pockets.

"You don't want to dance, do you?"

Of course, she said no.

Ten seconds later I was back in the boys' room. I was sure I was being rejected because the girls were embarrassed to dance with me. I looked into the mirror and bitterness welled up inside. Why me? Why did I have to be handicapped? What had I done wrong to deserve such punishment? I was angry, hurt, and felt terrible. I looked out and saw the other guys dancing with girls and I thought that it looked so easy for them. Then I looked up and saw my hands reflected. Suddenly, even the boys' room didn't seem like such a safe place — there were too many mirrors.

Then I remembered some advice Mom had given me. "If you want people to like you, put a smile on your face, take your hands out of your pockets, and stand very tall. If you want a girl to dance with you, you have to convince her this is something you really want to do."

I decided to give it one more try. From across the room, I saw a girl named Tammy Fryer. I knew her only slightly and she seemed like a very sweet girl, not as judgmental as some of the other kids. It wasn't as important to her that she danced with the quarterback of the football team. Once I got my nerve up, I made a beeline across the room. Had anybody gotten in my way, I probably would have run right over them. As I approached her, I took two deep breaths — my dad always told me to take two deep breaths before doing something important. I took my hands out of my pockets, put a smile on my face, and asked her to dance.

"Sure," she smiled back, "I'd love to dance with you."

And so we danced — my first dance.

The music was from the Saturday Night Fever album by the Bee Gees and I was inspired. I should add that in an effort to try and help me over my fear of dancing, my parents had given me several lessons. Both Mom and Dad love to dance and they would take turns dancing with me in the living room. So, once I hit the dance floor, I was feeling fairly confident. Saturday Night Fever was blaring from the speakers and like all the other guys, I wanted to dance like John Travolta, so I started spinning around with abandon. Pretty soon people began to back up — although I suspect it was more to get safely out of my way than it was to watch me. After awhile I had a pretty good audience. Tammy was having a great time and so was I.

I started spinning around on my left foot, which worked pretty well. My foot is so rigid that I could spin like crazy. I was spinning around and the other kids started yelling, "Go! Go!" when suddenly I heard a loud *SNAP!* I knew right away what had happened. The bolt that held my artificial leg and foot together had broken. Without that bolt, my foot stayed in one spot and my leg kept spinning around. I was rotating almost as fast as an ice skater in a tuck spin, and the kids went wild. "Wow!" they were yelling, "That guy can dance!"

When I finally stopped spinning, Tammy, who was laughing so hard she could hardly stand up, helped me over to a chair. I remember as we walked over, my foot was pointing in one direction and my leg another. It was easy to put the bolt back in place and before long I was back in action. I danced all night long. Not a single girl rejected my offer to dance the rest of the evening. To this day, Tammy Fryer insists I am the best dancer she's ever seen. I went to her wedding a few years ago and she told that story at the reception. "My husband's great," she said, "but he can't dance like Roger Crawford."

While I overcame my fear of dancing, I was still more than a little nervous about dating. After all, you had to touch if you went on a date, and I still was not sure how girls would react to my hands at close quarters. I didn't have my first date until the end of my sophomore year. To my surprise, I had caught the attention of a freshman named Wendy. She was a cheerleader and had blond hair and she sent her girl-friend over to tell me she wanted to go out with me. It's lucky she was so aggressive because I was still very shy around girls. In fact, I thought my friends were playing a joke on me at first. It took a lot of convincing before I realized that Wendy really did want to go out with me. Then, I got so nervous I couldn't sleep at night.

I'd always had a number of platonic relationships, but if a girl ever showed any romantic interest, I'd shy away. I couldn't figure out why any girl would want to go out with me when there were so many "normal" guys around.

On our first date we went for hamburgers and milkshakes at the local greasy spoon. But afterwards, we went to her house and her parents weren't around. We sat next to each other on the couch and talked. Suddenly, we looked into each other's eyes and it happened. I kissed her, or more accurately, she kissed me. It was my first kiss. It was long and passionate and finally we broke apart. I thought I was in heaven.

She gazed into my eyes.

I gazed back.

"Roger," she said. "Don't scrunch your lips up so much when you kiss."

I was stunned. I had practiced that kiss on my arm for two months and I thought I had it down. All this time I had been afraid that my physical handicaps would interfere with my relationship with girls. But the only criticism I had received about my first kiss was that I scrunched up my lips—and that part of my body was fully functional! I must add that I recovered well. I told her that I needed more practice and so we practiced away the afternoon on her parents' couch.

Wendy and I dated for a couple of months and I began to get over my fears of girls. However, there were still some awkward moments. Because I have difficulty holding small items, receiving change has always been a nightmare. I have to slide it with my right hand onto the back of my left hand, then try to work it into my pocket. It's so difficult for me that later on, when I had a summer job and commuted across the Oakland–San Francisco Bay Bridge to work, I asked the toll takers to toss my change into the car where I could pick it up later.

One of the first places Wendy and I went to was a movie. As luck would have it, the tickets cost $3.25 apiece, which meant I had 50 cents in change coming back. I tried to get it and dropped both quarters, which fell noisily to the ground and rolled to the feet of the couple standing in line behind us. I didn't even look at the money. There was no way I could pick it up. I took Wendy's arm and said, "Let's go." It worked out fine—Wendy was impressed that I was such a big spender.

But if Wendy gave me my first kiss, she also gave me my first heartbreak. Two months into our relationship Wendy fell in love with a wrestler. Apparently, he didn't scrunch up his lips when he kissed like I did. Our breakup was a real surprise to me because I figured I was going to marry Wendy. But she sent a friend over to tell me we were through. I was devastated. It reaffirmed all my old fears about my handicap—that no girl would want to stay with me. I moped around for almost a week before Dad called me in for a little talk.

"Roger," he said. "There are a lot of fish in the sea."

At first, our talk didn't help much because I was still convinced that Wendy was the only fish for me. But as I began to gain notoriety through tennis and began fitting into the mainstream of high school, my first heartache faded away.

By my senior year, girls were no longer intimidating and I was seeing a popular gal on campus, Cheryl Asterling. One night we had pizza with Ron and Ray and their dates and went on to the county fair. I kidded Ron and Ray after I knocked over the milk bottles at the baseball throwing booth and won a big stuffed bear for Cheryl. They both threw and missed. We ate cotton candy and wandered around the fairgrounds. Behind the rides was a long row of exhibits, including four large tents. A barker stood in front. He bragged that one of the tents held the world's fattest lady. Another tent contained a bearded lady and in a third was the world's shortest man. Large murals beside the tents depicted the people inside. We strolled past the three tents and stopped in front of the last tent. Inside was "Lobster Man." On the mural was a man whose hands looked like lobster claws. They were similar to mine. I dropped my cotton candy and thought I was going to be sick. I turned to Cheryl, who hadn't yet seen the mural, and told her I had to go home. She didn't understand. I screamed that I had to go home and she backed away from me.

"I'm not ready to go," she said.

My throat constricted. I just walked away toward the car.

Ron and Ray, who were laughing at the pictures, saw the "Lobster Man" mural and stopped laughing.

Cheryl waved a quick goodbye to them and ran

after me. On the way to the car, she kept asking me what was wrong and I wouldn't answer. I drove as fast as I could to her house because I didn't want to break down in tears in front of her, although that's what I should have done for both of our sakes. I dropped her off at her door and zoomed around the block where I pulled over and cried. I couldn't get the vision of "Lobster Man" in the freak show out of my mind. I felt sorry for the man, but I was angry, too. How could he do that to himself? To me?

I never had the courage to explain to Cheryl what had happened, though she learned from Ron and Ray. My unwillingness to talk about my insecurities doomed our relationship and Cheryl started dating other guys.

Second Serve

We will become what we imagine ourselves to be. This self-appraisal determines whether we see ourselves as winners or losers. Our *mental images* decide either self-limitations or boundless potential, while all of our actions and emotions are produced from our *self-images*. Therefore, if we believe we are failures, we will inevitably find ways to fail. Even if we have an opportunity for achievement, our negative self-images will become self-fulfilling prophecies.

We need to see ourselves as valuable, unique human beings. We all enter this world as originals, yet all too often we strive to be carbon copies.

We are not perfect—no one is. To gain healthy self-esteem, we must realize that we should strive to change what we can. It is important to acknowledge that some aspects of our lives need to be changed, but that we *can* accept ourselves as we are. When I realized that my hands were not perfect, but that they were *my* hands, my self-esteem began to improve because I was accepting what I couldn't change.

We all need to periodically conduct a self-appraisal—take an honest and careful look at our lives. We should each begin by asking ourselves, "What is uniquely positive about me?" Write the answer down, internalize it, and it will create internal boldness.

Chapter Nine

Learning to Drive

Ever since I learned to drive, I've noticed that people get nervous when they see me pull the car keys out. Even my wife, Donna, admitted to being a little tense when we first went for a spin with me at the wheel.

But of all the people who have ridden with me over the years, nobody was more nervous than the woman who gave me my first driving test. I was a junior at Monte Vista and I had already gained a temporary permit through my driver's training class at school. But to get my official license, so I could drive without my parents, I had to take the driver's test at the California Department of Motor Vehicles office. I was so excited that I didn't sleep a wink the night before. Being able to drive a car was a major social step in high school and I was especially looking forward to it because possessing a driver's license meant that I was equal to the other kids — some of whom had expressed doubts that I could drive a car.

My parents had no such doubts. In fact, they had already let me buy a used car. It was a sleek green Ford Fairlane with moon wheel rims that were so shiny you could actually see your face in them. I thought it was a mean street machine. (It was the car my dad later repossessed after I broke my end of our contract, but at that time I had no idea I'd end up losing it.) On the big day, my parents drove me to the DMV office where I had to fill out the usual lengthy paperwork. The entire time I was writing, the driving examiner, a portly lady with a worried look on her face, was hovering over me watching me write. I'm sure she was thinking, "Oh great, I've got to get in a car with a kid with no hands!"

After I completed the forms, she asked me to pull the car around so we could go out for my driving test. I was shaking. It was a cool October day, but I was sweating like mad. I pulled the car up in front of the DMV office and the driving examiner got in. She buckled up and looked at me skeptically.

"Are you sure you can drive?" she asked.

"No, but this is a good time to learn," I cracked with a straight face.

She looked down at my hands, then up at me and I smiled. She laughed and said, "Put it in drive and let's go."

I was so nervous I shoved it into reverse and we shot backwards for a few feet before I slammed on the brakes. After we bounced off the seat a few times, I looked over and noticed that her eyes had widened considerably. For a moment, I thought she was going to break and run for it, but she hung in there and we eventually made it around the block. I wouldn't say I passed the test with flying colors, but despite my shaky start I managed to avoid further catastrophes and she gave me a passing grade. Maybe she just didn't want to have to test me again, but I finally had my license!

I acted cool in front of my parents as I drove them back to our house. But later that day, Mom let me take the car out by myself. I immediately drove to the high school and went around the circular drive-way about 10 times. I kept going around and around and around, honking my horn and waving to people. I was sure that life couldn't get any better than that! The next day, though, I found out it could get a lot worse.

That night my father asked me to sit on the couch with him and he gave me the only rule regarding my car. "Roger, don't let anybody else drive your car — ever."

I said, "Dad, don't worry."

The following morning I parked my car in the school lot and was heading to my first class when a classmate came running up to me and said, "Roger, I need to borrow your car." He told me he had to go up the street about a mile to get some homework that he had forgotten at his house.

"You're the only person I know that has a car," he pleaded.

It happened that the boy was a very popular fellow on campus and I was flattered that he asked to borrow *my* car. Forgetting all about my father's warning, I flipped him the keys. To make a long story short, he didn't even make it out of the parking lot. Backing up, he turned too quickly and smacked right into an old Ford that was parked next to my car. The whole side of the Fairlane was dented and scraped.

The boy tossed me the keys, muttered an apology, and walked away. I sat down on the curb and cried. I was sure Dad was going to kill me when I got home.

As the day dragged on, I began to wonder what I was going to tell my parents. I thought about lying. Since the other car hadn't been damaged, I could say my car just got hit in the parking lot by an unknown driver. But I had always been honest with my parents, and I knew a lie would just make me feel lousier than I already did. Also, I hoped that since it was my 16th birthday that day, I would receive a little leniency.

I had planned to tell them right away about the car, but as I drove home, I lost a little of my nerve. I parked the car in front of our house so the dented side wouldn't show. I decided to delay telling my parents until after the birthday party they were throwing for me — I didn't want to ruin the whole party for them, or for me. The festivities went as planned, except my parents couldn't figure out why I didn't eat any birthday cake. Little did they know my stomach was churning so much I couldn't even think about eating!

Finally, when the last guest left, I told my dad about the car.

"Roger," he said, laughing and slapping me on the back. "Don't joke about a thing like that."

"Dad, I'm not joking."

His face tightened and went a little white around the corners. We went outside to survey the damage. He looked at the car and without looking at me, walked back into the house. I was miserable. Just then

I heard the telephone ring and Dad answered it. After talking for a few minutes, he hung up and called me into the house. As luck would have it, the father of the boy who crashed my car had called to apologize for his son and said he would pay for the damage. Dad still wasn't very happy—I soon was on the receiving end of a very stern lecture—but he hoped I had learned my lesson. As it turned out, I would lose the car before finally learning that regardless of how much I wanted to be accepted by my peers, I had to stick to my commitments.

During the summer after my sophomore year in high school, I decided to get a job. I needed spending money and I wanted to prove to myself I could get a job just like the other kids. I checked the want ads and spotted an opening for a stock boy at a local department store. I called the manager and we chatted for awhile on the phone and he asked me to come in for an interview. He said I sounded like someone he'd like to hire. I dressed up in a suit and tie and went in for the interview. The manager was busy at a different part of the store when I first got there, so his secretary told me to wait in his office. In five minutes, he returned. He burst into his office with a big smile and he put his hand out to say hello. But, when I put my hand out, his face dropped like a stone and he recoiled abruptly.

"I'm sorry," he said. "It's just that you didn't sound handicapped on the phone."

I didn't know whether to laugh or cry. I didn't *sound* handicapped? What did that mean?

Without asking me any further questions, or even asking me to sit down, he told me I wasn't right for the job and he showed me the door.

I was crushed and angry. I had been turned down before I even had a chance to show what I could do!

Something that I've run into much more than such outright prejudice, though, is the misconception about handicapped people. For example, many people tend to associate my deformed hands with a lack of intelligence. They figure since I'm physically impaired, I must be mentally deficient as well. It remains one of the great battles I have to fight. To this day, if I stop at a gas station to ask directions, some people will give them to me in a very loud voice and they will talk very slowly. I'm often tempted, after they've stood there and talked to me as if I were six years old, to tell them I have a BA in communications and that I might be able to help them with their speech problem.

Another common misconception about handicapped people is the unlikely idea that we all must know each other. I still have people come up to me when they see my hands and say, "Well, you must know Joe Blow in Montana because he's in a wheelchair," or, "Of course, you know Sally from Florida, she's blind." They must figure all handicapped folks go to the same parties and belong to the same clubs. I still can't quite figure that one out, but it happens a lot.

As I went through high school and was exposed to different types of people, I learned that the toughest part of having a handicap isn't the physical inconveniences—it's trying to deal with people's reactions to you. That is especially true for me because of my hands. Our hands are important communication tools. For example, when you meet people, the first thing you do is shake their hand. Historically, one of the very symbols of masculinity in our society is the firm handshake. Try as I might, I have never figured out how to produce a firm handshake from a hand that only has one finger! Even more difficult for me was the knowledge that one of the most important moments between lovers is the moment they touch. Who would want to touch my hands? I was afraid, and almost convinced, that no one ever would.

As a child, I hated the television commercials that showed closeups of two hands coming together. I got it in my head that, if I ate a lot of vitamins, my fingers would grow back. Mom didn't know why I wanted so many vitamins, but she was happy to see me take them.

It took some time to recover from my first job interview, but I was still determined to find work. I decided to try another department store, Emporium Capwell, which had advertised in the newspaper for a stockboy. I answered the ad and was asked to come in for an interview. I met the manager, John Cagneau. I was anxious, but after meeting John for the first time, I knew things were going to be okay. The first thing he said to me was, "I don't care what your hands or your leg looks like—what I care about is, can you lift a box?"

"You bet," I said excitedly and we went down to the stock room where I lifted the biggest box I could find. I also showed him how I could use a hand truck and how I could pick up a television.

"You start Monday," he said.

I thanked him politely, but on the way home I whooped and yelled so loud the neighbors must have thought I had lost my marbles.

That night I had a dream that is recurring. I have ten fingers and ten toes. I can pick things up with one hand and I actually can feel the sensation of grasping, even though in my conscious life I have never been able to do that. I like to think that this is an extension of the way I view myself—as an equal in an able-bodied world.

My job at Emporium Capwell went fine, but despite the fact that I never broke anything, there were a lot of people who began to worry when they saw me handling valuable merchandise, especially if the merchandise was their own. One afternoon I was working on the loading dock, when a call came through that a customer had purchased a large color television. My orders were to take the TV to the loading dock, where the customer would pick it up in his car.

As it happened, the television sets were loaded on a high shelf above the portable loading dock. I had to climb a ladder about ten feet off the ground to get it. It was no problem for me, I had done it a dozen times before. As I began lifting the TV off the shelf, the customer, a small Chinese man, drove around and parked by the loading dock. He saw me perched on the ladder with his TV and he saw my hands. He started to run toward me, yelling in Chinese. I wasn't paying much attention to him, however, because somebody had rolled the loading dock up against the ladder and I was trying to figure out how to get down the last two steps. No problem, I thought. I'll just jump.

The Chinese man saw what I was going to do and he came tearing around the loading dock; he was going to try to catch me and his TV! Luckily, he was a slow runner and I jumped before he could get there. I made a smooth landing and handed his TV to him with a smile. His eyes were wide and he was breathless when he took it. I was just glad he didn't know I had an artificial leg, too!

୬ଈ

Getting the job at the department store was a real boost to my self esteem. I was lifting heavy boxes and moving them around—I felt it was a real man's job. Later, that macho idea got me into a little trouble. I had been at the store for a couple of months and I was really feeling my oats. There wasn't any box too big or too heavy for me to lift, or so I thought.

That notion came to a sudden end one day when I was in the housewares department stacking up boxes of fine china. I was putting all the boxes on a pallet, which I was going to pull back to the warehouse. As it turned out, I put so many boxes on the pallet it took all my strength just to move it. I was pulling with all my might when I turned my artificial leg wrong and it snapped completely in half. I went skidding across the floor on my back and my foot scooted the other way, right by several startled customers. They all looked at me in horror and I couldn't help but laugh. After I assured them I was okay, another clerk called John Cagneau and told him I had broken my leg. John came running, thinking I was really hurt. Then he saw me, sitting with a box of fine china in my lap, holding my foot.

"Don't ever do that to me again!" he said, but then he laughed, too. I called home for my other leg and I worked the rest of the afternoon. But I was careful, from that day on, never to fill my boxes too full.

Second Serve

I am often asked, "Is holding your tennis racket with your right finger tightly wedged between two metal bars painful?" I reply that the only time I feel discomfort is when I take my eye off the ball.

Isn't this true in all of our lives? We see problems when we take our eyes off the purpose. Exactness of purpose is the hallmark of achievement. It fortifies the courage needed to face life's struggles. Keeping our eyes on the ball will give us the determination to carry on until we succeed.

Chapter Ten

Apartment 101: Making the Grade at Loyola

Although I professed to my friends that I was excited about our upcoming graduation from Monte Vista, I was apprehensive.

During our high school graduation ceremony, I can remember looking up into the audience with a sinking feeling in my stomach. I was about to leave my comfort zone. Everybody knew me in the school and I could walk around without my hands in my pockets. I knew I wanted to go on to college, but that meant a whole new regimen of questions, stares, and faces.

I had maintained a "B" average throughout high school, but I wasn't sure which university I wanted to attend. In California, the community college system is excellent, so I decided to attend nearby Diablo Valley Community College while I sorted out my next move.

The only thing I knew for sure was that I wanted to continue to play tennis. Although most people assumed my career was over, Tony Fisher and I had other ideas. I taught tennis at Crow Canyon Country Club near Danville, and to make spending money I continued to work at the department store.

At Diablo Valley, I became more interested in academics than I had been in high school, because I had begun to realize that I was going to have to make a living after I got out of college.

As a result, my two years at Diablo Valley were very stimulating academically. I went from being a "B" student in high school to an "A" student in college. One of my favorite classes was an English literature course taught by Dr. Clark Sturges. It was during this class that I first read *Of Human Bondage* by W. Somerset Maugham. The book had a tremendous impact on me. The story revolves around the character Phillip Carey, a handicapped orphan. I identified closely with Carey because he had to deal with the same things I did—the stares, the questions, and the cutting comments—while he struggled with his self esteem. Maugham, who had a club foot himself, did a wonderful job of showing what it is like to be handicapped, to be different. I saw a lot of myself in Phillip Carey and it was a great revelation for me when Carey came to understand that his handicap was only a minor inconvenience. The real problem he faced was his own feelings of insecurity.

Toward the end of my second year, I enrolled in another English class and found myself sitting next to an extraordinary man. His name was Bob and he was 80 years old. He was short and always wore a white shirt, baggy dark pants, and a baseball cap. Bob and I struck up a friendship and we regularly ate lunch together in the school cafeteria. He told me stories of his life and he shared some of his triumphs and regrets. His dream had always been to get a college education, but he had bowed to family pressure and gone to work immediately after high school. Soon he had a wife and family and only now, at 80 years old, did he have the opportunity to achieve his dream.

One of his lifelong ambitions was to write a book. As he got older, he began to realize he didn't have enough strength left to write an entire book, so he wrote an article for the Diablo Valley school newspaper instead. The article was about our special friendship and what it meant to him. I was saddened when Bob died, just weeks after the article was published. His life and his death had a great effect on me. At night, I'd think about his words. "Don't wait on your dreams," he would say, "because your dreams won't wait for you. Time has a way of speeding up as you get older, so act now. And live every day to the fullest, because you're trading a day of your life for it."

One of the classes I took at Diablo Valley was a beginning speech class. I had taken it because I needed to fill up my schedule, but though I didn't have much self confidence when it came to public speaking (my knees shook so badly that for my first couple of speeches I had to stand behind a lectern), I found I liked it. Through the encouragement of Paul Phalin, my speech professor, I took two other speech classes before I graduated. The fun I had in those classes helped convince me that I wanted to try public speaking as a career and I established a major in communications.

After graduating from Diablo Valley, I was offered tennis scholarships to nearly a dozen universities and I took some time to make my choice. I didn't have to worry about finances because I also received the Porter Scholarship Award from Diablo Valley, which is given for athletic and scholastic abilities, and a scholarship from the State Department of Rehabilitation, for handicapped people who are trying to help themselves.

One of the collegiate tennis coaches I had talked to was Jamie Sanchez at Loyola Marymount in Los Angeles, and he invited me to LMU for a tryout. Dad and I drove down during the summer and I immediately fell in love with the campus. It is located on a beautiful hilltop overlooking Marina Del Rey near the Pacific Ocean. Loyola has one of the top-rated communications departments in the country and the school was small enough so I didn't feel I'd get lost in the crowd. It was also far enough away from home that I could get a taste of independence, yet close enough that I could drive back whenever I had a break.

I was also excited because the tennis team played in the West Coast Athletic Conference, one of the better collegiate tennis conferences in the country.

During the summer before I left for school, I had one minor setback that may go down as the most unusual tennis injury ever recorded. I was working out twice a day with Tony and playing hours and hours of tennis. Late in the summer I started to suffer from back pain and it continued to get worse. Finally, it got so bad that I went to a doctor. I was surprised when he pulled out a tape measure and examined my legs. He found that my artificial leg was an inch shorter than my real leg. That meant I was coming down so hard on my right leg that it was causing muscle spasms in my back. I was shocked because I had not grown at all since I was in 7th grade. All of a sudden I had grown an inch! When I ordered a new prosthesis, I found the doctor was right. The new leg was an inch longer and my back problems disappeared.

$\approx$

As the summer ebbed, I began to get more and more excited about going to school at Loyola, especially after I got a letter from the school saying I was going to receive on-campus housing. I was thrilled because there was a very limited amount of on-campus apartment space. The letter said I had been assigned to Apartment 101.

The day before I left for school my dad and I were packing up the car when he turned and hugged me and told me he would miss me. Suddenly it really dawned on me that I was about to leave home for good. The night before we left, I couldn't sleep. The next morning Dad reminded me to keep my hands out of my pockets, my chin up, and a smile on my face. He again stressed that it was my responsibility to make sure people felt comfortable with my handicaps. I can remember wondering why he was giving me all that advice; after all, I was 19 years old and I knew everything.

When we finally arrived at Loyola, we began to look for my apartment. We walked all over campus and saw all the other apartment numbers, but Apartment 101 was not to be found. Finally, we walked to the very back edge of the campus and there it was. A wheelchair ramp led to the front door. Immediately, my stomach started churning. I thought, "Oh no, they've put me in a handicapped apartment." I avoided the wheelchair ramp and walked down the stairs. I knocked, then opened the door and bumped right into my new roommate. His name was Chris Senden and he was blind. I turned to my right and rammed my shins into my other roommate. His name was Daniel Barnes and he was in a wheelchair. I was stunned and my stomach was doing jumping jacks. *They had put all the handicapped students together and I was one of them.* Daniel looked at me and stuck out his hand.

"Welcome to the dungeon," he said simply.

I didn't know what to say so I excused myself and walked out to get my stuff in the car. This time I walked up the wheelchair ramp.

I kept thinking to myself, "I thought I had come so far. I thought nobody would ever label me disabled again. I've become a tennis player, I've received a scholarship to go to college, and now this. They put me in a handicapped apartment." I was devastated, not because I had to bunk with Chris and Daniel (they turned out to be great guys), but because the school had labeled me *disabled*.

I was crying with anger as I walked past the rows of apartments, through the parking lot, and up to the office of the housing director. The director was very nice. He calmed me down and, in response to my question, explained that all students who marked the "Are you handicapped?" box on their application were put in the same apartments. I rarely check the handicapped box on applications, but this time I did because I had to explain about my state scholarship. I told him I wanted to be moved. He said there was only one possible vacancy left and gave me directions. I went there and knocked on the door and a young man appeared. I told him my plight, shook his hand, and asked him if he had a spare room. He said no, and shut the door. Later, he and I became friends and he admitted that there had indeed been a vacancy, but he had been apprehensive and felt I would have difficulty fitting in. We've since laughed about it over beer and pizza, but it's a memory I still carry.

I walked back to the car and told Dad I wanted to go home. He knew what I was feeling and he told me we should go get something to eat before we made any decisions. I was so upset that over dinner I couldn't hold back the tears. Dad put his arm around me.

I was saddened because it became very clear to me that regardless of what I accomplished in my life, I had no control over the labels that other people put on me. The school administration had labeled me and there wasn't a thing I could do about it.

Dad reminded me that I could control the labels I put on myself. He said quitting school wasn't an option for me and that it was up to me to prove to the people at Loyola what I could do. The important labels were the ones I applied to myself.

Grudgingly, I moved my stuff into Apartment

101 and got my room together. I shook hands with
Daniel. Chris felt my hands, my face and my artificial
leg. It was his way of getting to know me.

The next day I awoke in a gloomy mood and
wandered down to the student union to get some
breakfast. When I got there, I felt like everybody was
staring at me. "Sure," I felt them thinking. "We know
who that guy is, he lives in Apartment 101."

I was feeling pretty low when a tall, athletic guy
with long hair and a rock'n'roll t-shirt came up to me
and said, "Hi, I'm John Crowley. I play on the tennis
team. You must be Roger. Glad to know ya."

John shook my hand and sat down. As it turned
out, he was the number one player on the team and
we talked about tennis for an hour. He told me all
about the Loyola tennis squad and about the school.
By the time we were finished talking, my gloom had
disappeared and my spirits were rising. Suddenly, a
human face was emerging out of the impenetrable
mass of this university, and I started to feel like I
might fit in after all.

Over the next few months I had a chance to get
to know my roommate Daniel. He had been para-
lyzed when he was struck by a car. Before the accident, he had been a good athlete and was very active
physically. The injury left him a quadraplegic,
confined to a wheelchair. I also got to know Chris,
who had been blind since birth. The three of us spent
hours sitting around the kitchen table talking about
facing life with a disability. Through our discussions
I found something that was comforting in a way—we
all had the same fears about the future. Perhaps the
greatest fear we each had was whether we would ever

find someone to marry. How could we compete against able-bodied guys?

We also talked about our mutual problem of being accepted in able-bodied society, but Daniel and Chris had specific problems I hadn't thought about before. They both had access difficulties. I had always taken my ability to drive a car for granted, but talking with them made me realize how difficult it would be not to be able to drive. Also, Chris had limited mobility because of his lack of sight and Dan because of his wheelchair. For example, whenever we went out to eat, we had to find a restaurant that had a table high enough that Daniel could get his wheelchair under it.

We also talked about how difficult it was for Daniel to adjust to his limitation, since he wasn't born with it. It was much harder for him to deal with his setback than it was for Chris and me, who had been born with our handicaps.

Though we shared a common ground, we also agreed that we didn't want to live together . . . not because we didn't like each other, but because we felt branded. But we were stuck with each other for the first six months and we were determined to make the best of it.

We helped each other out as much as we could. For example, one day Daniel had to go across the city to the University of Southern California for an exam. He asked me to drive him, so I wheeled him out, picked him up and put him in the passenger seat, folded his chair, and we drove to USC. Once we found the hall where the test was to be held, I pulled into the handicapped parking zone. Classes had just been let out and there were students everywhere. I opened Daniel's door and put one arm under his knees and the other under his arms. I picked him up and put him in his wheelchair. Since Daniel is 6'2" tall, it wasn't an easy task. When I was done, a student came up to me and looked at my leg (I was wearing shorts). He said: "You know something, when you pulled up, I thought you were going into the wheel-chair and he was going to push you."

Over the next few months, I began to appreciate my roommates' humor. Roommate pranks are pretty standard fare in college, but when you live with a guy who's blind and another in a wheelchair, the pranks can get really interesting. For example, if Chris would do something that annoyed us, like forget to do the dishes when it was his turn, we'd rearrange the furniture without telling him. As soon as he'd bump into the first chair, he'd know what had happened and he'd laugh and promise to get at the dishes right away. When Daniel would shirk his duties around the apartment, Chris and I would build barricades so he couldn't get his wheelchair out of the hall. And the two of them would hide my artificial leg if I did something they didn't like.

After we had been in Apartment 101 for a few months, we decided to have a party. This wasn't a little block party or even an apartment-wide party . . . we threw the biggest campus-wide bash of the year. Word spread around the college like wildfire and our party became the event of the season. Hundreds of people showed up and the party spilled out of our packed apartment into the lawn below. The party rocked on all night long and by the time it wound down in the wee hours of the morning I felt as though I had met most of the kids on campus. The party proved to be a catalyst for all three of us in good old Apartment 101. People seemed more relaxed around us after that and everybody called us by our first names. That was a great feeling for all three of us.

We still faced some unique problems, though. For example, if something dropped to the floor and I couldn't pick it up, nobody could. And household repairs sometimes turned into a comedy of errors. One night the pipe under the sink sprung a leak and it was too late to call the apartment maintenance people. We had to fix it ourselves. It took all three of us to do it. Since there was still some water squirting out of the pipe, I took Chris' finger and put it over the leak. Daniel wedged his wheelchair under the sink so I had something to hang onto as I tried to wrestle with the pipe. He handed me the tools as I needed them. It took us almost an hour, but working together, we managed to fix the leak.

Another time a friend of mine called the apartment and asked Chris if I was home. Chris said he thought I was sleeping and he walked into my bedroom to check. I was out on the tennis court at the time, but I had left my walking leg on the bed. Chris felt my leg on the bed and told my friend that I was sleeping soundly.

One night, a few months before the semester ended, Daniel, Chris, and I were asleep when I heard the front door opening. I got up, put on my artificial leg, and peeked out my door. I could see three guys I didn't know, unplugging Daniel's television. Even in the dim light I could see these were big men and I should have been scared. But instead, a rage built up inside me. These guys obviously knew the three of us had disabilities and the cowardice of their actions made me boil over. I doubled up my fists as best as I could and bolted out the door. The guy nearest me stood up with a look of disbelief on his face. I swung at him as hard as I could. I meant to smack him in the jaw, but instead I stuck him right in the eye with my finger. He howled in pain and fell to the floor. I went after the other two guys — but I stepped right into a left hook and stars exploded around the room. I stayed on my feet, though, and charged them again. I grabbed one of them by the neck, but the other guy pulled me off and all three of them started hitting and kicking me. One punch landed on my temple and I went out like a light.

I learned later that as the three thugs ran out of the apartment, they also beat up two of my neighbors who had come down to see what was going on.

I woke up in the darkness and crawled over to the phone and called the police. They came and took down our statements, but the three assailants were never caught. However, by the next day, word of the assaults had spread around campus. People started calling and stopping by to see how I was. Everybody thought I was pretty heroic for putting up a fight, but I didn't feel heroic. I had a fat lip, a black eye, a swollen nose, and some very sore ribs.

Daniel, Chris, and I were stunned by what had happened. But it taught us a sobering lesson. There are people out there who will take advantage of anybody they can, regardless of whom they hurt. These are ruthless people, out for their own gain, and they have no morals, no ethics, and no regard for human life. I choose not to dwell on this vicious and mean element in our society, but that experience left me with a wiser, if sadder, understanding of the world.

Just before the second semester began, I moved into another apartment with some friends on the tennis team and I began to feel at home on the Loyola campus. I wore shorts every day.

Although I was keeping a B + average in school, I was really focused on playing tennis. When tryouts began, Coach Sanchez made it very clear that no one was assured a position on the team. Coach Sanchez is a big, burly guy, who played football at Loyola and is an excellent athlete. He has a big black beard and is a very intimidating figure, but as we came to learn, he is a gentle giant. He is a sensitive, compassionate man and a terrific coach. Before tryouts began he took me aside and told me that each player was going to be judged on how well they played, not on how they looked. That made me feel good and I was determined to give it my best shot.

The first day on the courts, John Crowley asked me to hit with him. Since John was the number one guy on the team it gave me a lot of confidence when he singled me out. I needed it, because about 60 guys were swarming around the courts... and only 12 of us were going to make the team.

That afternoon we started the challenge matches to determine who would make the squad. It was a nerve-wracking week for me because it was a round robin tournament where I had to compete against several players. But I was on my game and I kept winning until 40 players were eliminated and only 20 players remained. Still, just 12 of us were going to make the team. That meant I had to win one more match. I was feeling confident until I learned that I was paired against a top Swiss player who was an exchange student at Loyola. I hadn't competed against many foreign players and I was unsure how strong his game would be. I had come so close to making the team, and now this.

I called Tony Fisher and asked for advice on how to play against a clay court player. Tony told me that I had to have patience, that clay court players are not usually aggressive and are used to long rallies. That gave me some confidence because the strength of my game is patience—hitting the ball over the net one more time than the other guy.

The Swiss player and I had a long, intense match, but I managed to beat him 6–4 in the final set. I was thrilled, but I also felt sorry for him. Soon after the match, he packed his clothes and flew back to Switzerland. I often wonder how much our match had to do with his departure.

I was excited that I had made the team. It was a dream come true and I was especially proud when the people in the athletic department told me that I was the first severely handicapped athlete in the National Collegiate Athletic Association's history ever to earn a varsity letter in tennis, or any other college sport. I am still the only severely (all four limbs affected) handicapped player in NCAA history to earn a letter in a Division One sport.

Other handicapped athletes, who have had one limb affected, have since broken through to play for

NCAA Division One teams, most notably baseball pitcher Jim Abbott. Abbott, who played for the gold-medal winning 1988 Olympic baseball team and now plays for the California Angels in the major leagues, has received a great deal of publicity for his achievements, and I think that is wonderful. That kind of publicity not only makes able-bodied people aware that handicapped people can succeed in athletics, it also inspires those who are physically challenged.

I had a number of positive experiences playing tennis for Loyola, but none was more memorable than our team's trip to Mexico. We traveled for a couple of weeks throughout the country and we played exhibition matches with various university teams. We went to a number of cities including Mexico City, Acapulco, and Cuernavaca. While we were on our trip, I began to notice that people were eyeing me strangely. I asked one of the coaches on the team, who had once lived in Mexico, why everybody was staring at me. The coach told me that in Mexico, handicapped people are not generally treated well and many of them end up on the streets as beggers. The fact that I walked around in nice clothes and was on the tennis team was astonishing to them, he said.

One morning in Mexico City I got up early and went jogging in Chepultipec Park. I was running around the park when I ran past a school yard. I was wearing my tennis outfit and I was deep in a running trance when suddenly I was startled by the appearance of two dozen children. They had run out of the school yard and began chasing me. They were yelling things at me in Spanish, which I didn't understand. I didn't know what was going on, so I just smiled back at them and kept running. But the kids kept up with me and sometimes they would run up and try to touch me. Finally, I stopped by my hotel and the kids all crowded around me trying to touch my artificial leg. I was bewildered, but they seemed friendly enough. Just then, a member of the women's team, Carolyn Partridge, came walking by. Carolyn spoke Spanish, so I asked her to tell me what the children were shouting. I thought they were laughing at me.

"They're cheering for you," Carolyn said. "They've never seen anybody like you before. Most of the handicapped people they know beg on the street."

Just then, the children's teacher caught up with us and spoke to Carolyn in Spanish.

"He says you are courageous," she translated. "And he says, 'Keep it up, keep it up.'"

I looked at these little kids rubbing my leg and tears welled up in my eyes. I didn't know whether the tears were for these little children and the joy they had brought me, or whether it was for all those unfortunate broken souls begging on street corners all over the world.

But one thing I know for sure. I'll never forget the promise I saw in those little faces. I like to think it was the promise that someday, all people will get a fair opportunity in their lifetime — even if they're born imperfect.

Chapter Eleven

A Leg Up on "Good Morning America"

My senior year of tennis at Loyola began with a bang. A representative from the television show "Good Morning America" called me at my apartment and said they wanted to do a segment on me for the show. They had seen an article on me that appeared in the *New York Times* and thought my story would be of interest to their viewers. Tony Fisher coordinated everything for me with the television producers and was instrumental in making the whole thing happen. The producers decided to send out Los Angeles-based, free-lance reporter Tom Sullivan to do the piece. Tom was doing a number of remote spots for the show at the time. Tom is an ace reporter. He's also blind.

Tom had the cameras follow me around campus,

showing me on a "normal" day. The cameraman also tagged along when I went into the locker room to get ready for a tennis match. Tom had asked me earlier if I minded if they got a shot of my left leg without my prosthesis on. It was a tough decision for me. Showing my stump to a close friend was difficult enough; showing it to millions of viewers was something else again. But I did it in the locker room as I was getting ready for a match. It all seemed quite natural on film—I slipped the artificial leg and my sock off, then put on my tennis socks and pulled my leg back on. It took only a minute, but it had an amazing impact. After the show aired, I received scores of letters from people all over the United States. One of them was addressed simply to: "Handicapped Tennis Player, Los Angeles, CA, USA" and the Post Office forwarded it on to me.

Many of the letters were from able-bodied people, thanking me for erasing their curiosity. Most of them had known somebody with a missing limb and were very curious about what it looked and felt like to be handicapped.

Many other letters were from Vietnam War veterans who had lost a limb in battle. Most of them thanked me for showing my leg. They said by exposing it on national television it was as if I had taken their own fears out of the closet and allowed them to evaporate in the light of day. Many of them said it was the first time they had ever seen an amputee take a prosthesis off on the air.

Later in the year, the producers of a TV show called, "Kids Are People, Too" contacted me and asked me to appear on their show in New York. It sounded like fun, so I accepted their kind offer and flew back to New York. I was given the red carpet treatment and had a terrific time.

Following those shows, I was fortunate enough to appear on a number of other national television shows, including "Real People," "Great Space Coaster," and "You Asked For It." I also played a part in the television movie "In a New Light," which subsequently won an Emmy Award.

By the time I flew home to Loyola, I had become well-known around campus. Students I didn't know were coming up to me and introducing themselves and I was on top of the world. In fact, I became a little self-absorbed. Phil, a good friend of mine from high school, came to visit me during this time. I hadn't seen him for three years and I was anxious to impress him with the changes in my life. We went out for pizza and I talked nonstop about my accomplishments. I didn't realize it at the time, but poor Phil didn't get a word in edgewise. I felt good about his visit until I received a letter from him two weeks later. It began: "Dear Roger, I wanted to share with you some advice that only a friend can give." Phil went on to tell me that I was so preoccupied with my own growth that I ignored everybody else. The years since high school had been tough for Phil and he had hoped to talk about some of his difficulties with me. I never gave him the chance. He copied a page out of the book, *How to Win Friends and Influence People* by Dale Carnegie. The title of the page was "How to deal with people who talk too much."

After I read the letter, I slammed it down on the table and called Phil some unprintable names. But I didn't throw it away. I kept it in my drawer and a few days later, after I cooled off, I pulled it out and read it carefully. I took a hard look at my relationships with people and I reluctantly admitted to myself that Phil was right. All the television shows and attention I had been receiving for my tennis had gone to my head. It was a valuable lesson.

Although I was interested in school and maintained my grades, tennis continued to be my primary focus. Loyola had always fielded a strong tennis squad and had one of the most challenging schedules in the nation. Coach Sanchez deserves a lot of credit for maintaining a strong program year after year. As a coach, he is a good teacher and a great motivator. He was instrumental in continually encouraging us to be our best. Although we weren't the best team in the WCAC, Jamie helped us maximize our abilities. He spent a lot of extra time working with me to develop strategies to overcome my lack of reach. My arms are short and the way I hold the racket causes me to lose another foot or two of extension that most able-bodied people have. Therefore, I had to develop unique strategies to keep the other player from exploiting my limitations. I had to hit a lot of slice and drop shots at the other players' feet so they couldn't work the outside lines on me. My quickness surprised most players. Many of them thought they could beat me by dropping a shot by the net, then lobbing the next one over my head. But I didn't have much trouble handling those shots; it was when I had to run from side to side that my lack of reach became evident.

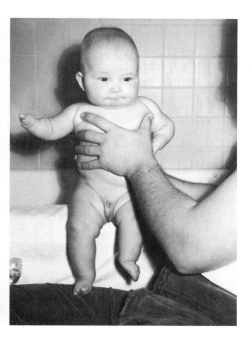

All of me at age six months.

Dad and I in 1961.

Mom and I on a family vacation in Kentucky.

My first fishing trip and my first fish! I'm not sure which one of us was more surprised.

"Power forward" for the Knicks at age 11. This was taken shortly before I scored the wrong way basket.

Having fun on our boat in the Salt Fork Lake in southern Ohio.

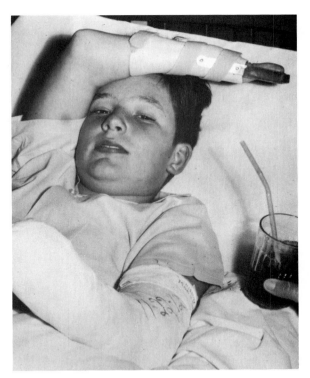

After surgery at the Shriner's Hospital. Doctors implanted the Achilles heel from my left foot into my left hand.

At age 14, showing off my first Wilson T-2000 racket.

Receiving the ''Northern California Sportsman of the Year'' award in 1978, with Raider football great Gene Upshaw.

Playing tennis for Loyola Marymount University at the Las Vegas Invitational.

My friend and tennis coach Tony Fisher and I fresh from filming a television show. Guess which one.

Family portrait. From right to left; Dad, Brian, Grandma Crawford, me, and Mom.

Starting my speaking career in 1985.

After a celebrity tennis match with 49er stars Freddie Solomon and Joe Montana. (Photo courtesy Gus Bower Photography.)

Donna and I on a special day.

Playing tennis near our home in Discovery Bay. (Photo courtesy of Gus Bower Photography.)

Donna and Alexa—the loves of my life.

The team enjoyed a good year. We won more matches than we lost in conference play. I played the fifth and sixth singles position and finished my career with a total of 22 wins and 11 losses.

We had a number of memorable matches, including one against Notre Dame University on St. Patrick's Day. Notre Dame was a powerhouse then and they beat us, but not without a struggle. Of all the matches I played, though, one of my favorites was against Iona University of New York. I was matched against a big strong player who had the kind of game that usually gave me trouble. He had a big serve, pinpoint accuracy on his volleys, and enough power to run me from side to side. I knew I was in for a long day.

To beat this player, I had to establish the baseline; that is, I had to keep him moving, rather than allow him to move me. I have an average serve and a decent volley, but my forehand is my best weapon. I had to establish it early to have a chance.

From the beginning of the match, we were both playing at the top of our games. He was hitting thunderous serves and I found the range with my forehand. I managed to gain control of the baseline early, primarily because he made the mistake of trying to hit drop-shots and lobs. He looked a little surprised when he realized I could run and jump off my artificial leg. After I put away a few short lobs, he abandoned that strategy and began to battle for supremacy of the baseline.

The match evened up after that and neither one of us was able to gain an advantage. We split the first two sets. The third match was going to decide the winner. Just before serving the third set, I told myself to focus on what I could control and ignore everything else. I tried to build a mental wall around the court and shut everything else out.

I was lucky enough to break his serve early and gain a slight advantage. Breaking his service rattled my opponent a little and I could tell he was starting to force his shots, trying to hit a winner every time. I remembered to relax and to be patient, to just hit it over the net one more time than he did. He hit some winners now and then, but he made even more mistakes and I wrapped up the match, 6–4, in the final set.

Since our match had taken so long, most of the other players were already finished with their matches and had come over to watch. They stood up and cheered both of us when the match was over. Being appreciated by your peers is the highest accolade.

A few minutes after the match my opponent walked over to me. I wasn't sure why, but my apprehensions were eased when he smiled and extended his hand. He patted me on the back.

"Would you sign my tennis cover?" he asked.

I laughed. "Sure."

Then he asked: "Will you send me a picture of yourself? I want to show everybody that this was the guy who beat the hell out of me and almost ended my tennis career."

That guy had a lot of style.

Before the fall semester started, I moved into an apartment with a couple of friends near the beach and we thought we were really living the L.A. lifestyle. I bought a beach bike — an old one-speed with big fat tires for riding on the sand — sunglasses, swimming trunks, and a lot of tanning oil. I figured that's all I'd need for the rest of the summer.

But, after a week of lolling around on the beach, I became restless and felt it was time to get a job. During my job search, I ran across a small card on the campus job bulletin board from the Los Angeles Crippled Children's Home. It said there was an opening for someone to work with the children as a counselor during the summer. It sounded promising.

I called the number on the card and talked to the director. One of the first questions he asked me was if I would have difficulty dealing with minority children. I assured him otherwise.

"I also think you should know that most of these kids are throw-aways," the director said.

"Throw-aways?" I didn't know exactly what the term meant, but a knot began twisting in my stomach.

"Basically, most of the children you'll be dealing with have been thrown away by their parents," he explained. "They have either been abandoned or shuffled off to foster homes. So, they not only have physical handicaps, they have emotional challenges as well."

I had the job when I hung up the phone, but I felt lousy.

My task at the children's center was to help coordinate activities with the kids, whose ages ranged from 8 to 16 years old. All of them had some type of physical disability, ranging from mild to severe. Most of them could play games like volleyball and ping-pong, but some of them could not. Before long I considered it my personal challenge to find at least one activity in which everyone could participate. In the case of Garrett, a ten-year-old boy, that was no simple task. Garrett was born without arms and legs. Garrett and I became friends and our relationship, which grew over the summer, came to have a great impact on my life.

I believe that those who suffer from severe handicaps are compensated in some other way. If that's true, then Garrett got his reward in the sparkle in his eye and in his gentle, sweet nature. It's hard to imagine why Garrett was so content—he was born at home and his parents didn't even take time to name him before they abandoned him in a neighborhood trash dumpster. But Garrett found joy in the life he lived. His spirit was indomitable.

Garrett stood with the aid of a large plastic cup-like device; he actually stood up inside of it. He had artificial legs, but they were new to him and he didn't wear them very often. Trying to find activities in which Garrett could participate was definitely my biggest challenge, for two reasons. First, of course, he was severely limited physically. Second, the other children made fun of him. You might think that when handicapped kids get together they are more sensitive to each other and don't tease. Unfortunately, that's not so. Garrett was the low man on the totem pole in terms of handicap severity and the other kids often taunted him. As a consequence, Garrett pulled inside himself when he was around them. He didn't say much, but I could tell he was suffering.

From their behavior, it was clear that the biggest

handicap these kids had was mental. The abuse all of them absorbed from their families had destroyed their self esteem and created reservoirs of distrust and hostility. Garrett, the most defenseless of them all, was the natural target.

I struggled for much of the summer to find something that Garrett could do with the other kids. All the typical activities, such as basketball and baseball, were out because Garrett simply had no way to participate. Finally, I had an idea. I went to the store to buy what I needed, then I put a big poster up on the center bulletin board. BUBBLE GUM BLOWING CONTEST AT 1 P.M., the poster said. Everybody was invited to compete.

I had to place the bubble gum in Garrett's mouth, but he was eager to start blowing, and soon enough we all found out why. Garrett could blow a bubble twice as big as anybody else. He was a bubble blowing machine. He could blow bubbles bigger than his head. They covered his face when they popped. I would pull the gum off his face and he'd be ready to blow another one. He won the contest going away and the kids all came over to congratulate him. Blowing those huge bubbles gave Garrett stature, much like my ability to sling dirt clods had won the grudging respect of Donnie Ponzoni years earlier. Garrett broke into a gigantic smile when I handed him his trophy—it was the first time I ever saw him smile around the other kids.

I wish I could say I had tremendous success with Garrett, but the truth was he pulled back into his contented shell after the bubble gum blowing contest. I left the center at the end of the summer, but I've never forgotten those kids. About four years later, I received a wonderful surprise in the mail. It was a letter from Garrett. He had learned to write by holding his pen between his chin and his shoulder. He wrote to tell me that he was fulfilling a class assignment to write to a friend who had made a difference in his life. He said "Hi" and wondered what I was doing. I wrote him back and told him I was proud that he had learned to write so well. Something tells me that Garrett will be okay.

My parents used to tell me: "The difference between a stumbling block and a stepping stone is six inches... between your ears."

❧

Late in the season, I went shopping for some new clothes in a large mall and two small children came up to me and began to ask me questions about my hands and my leg. Since I love children, I am always happy to answer their questions, but as I was about to tell them about my leg, their mother came up and screamed at them. She was embarrassed that they had asked me questions—she was the only one of the four of us that was—and she yanked the children away.

"That's not nice to ask people like that questions!" she hissed. Then she spanked them.

Her reaction—many parents have similar reactions—is exactly the opposite of what it should have been. Punishing kids for talking to a handicapped person was detrimental to me, as it is to every physically challenged person, because it gave the children the message that they should be afraid of us. Children have a natural curiosity and most handicapped people are happy to explain to them why they look different. It's a very hurtful thing to see a child spanked because he or she wanted to talk to you. That kind of parental reaction remains one of the toughest problems I have to face.

If I had one message to parents, it would be that most handicapped people are not insulted in the least by the curiosity of children. Most of us look forward to the opportunity of educating them as to why we look different. If I show them kindness and let them hold my hand or touch my leg, then hopefully when they see another person who is disabled they will look at them with understanding, not with fear or pity.

ã

During my last year at Loyola, I took a lot of communications and English lecture classes and that caused me some concern. I can't write very fast, and I had a lot of trouble taking notes in class. I didn't feel comfortable asking the professors to slow down, so I developed my own style of jotting down notes — I called it the Crawford Shorthand Technique. Nobody else could read my scribblings, though, and sometimes I couldn't even read them myself!

Because I was majoring in communications, there were a lot of papers required and most of them had to be typed. Since I can't type, I got around that by dictating my notes into a tape recorder and having them transcribed by a professional typist. But there were still in-class tests where writing was required and I had to struggle to keep up. Although I have to write with two hands, by the end of my senior year I had increased my writing speed enough so that I no longer had trouble with the pop quizzes during class.

છે.

My senior year was fun. My classes were exciting and I was playing good tennis. I was becoming more at ease around women and began dating an attractive classmate, Moura Bennet. We met at a beach volley-ball tournament and during the year our friendship turned romantic. We shared good times, though we eventually lost touch after she relocated to go to law school. It was the first mature relationship I'd had and it boosted my confidence.

Although institutions of higher learning are thought of as hallowed grounds, where one goes to ponder deep thoughts and explore esoteric lines of reasoning and logic, once in awhile a lesson of a strictly practical nature is likely to sneak by when you least expect. Such was the case when I dated a young lady, who used to come out to watch the tennis team practice. We struck up a friendship and after a couple of weeks I asked her out to dinner and a movie and she accepted. Since it wasn't time for me to do laundry yet, I had to borrow one of my roommate's clean shirts and I went to pick her up at her house. I knocked on the door and she answered ... and so did her dog. The dog, a huge monster that looked to me like a cross between a pit bull and a St. Bernard, was snarling and growling and straining at his leash to get at me.

"Why don't you come in for a drink?" my date said.

"Well, I don't know," I said with my eyes on the dog.

"Oh, he won't bite," she said.

I wasn't so sure.

Neither was the dog because the minute I stepped into the door it lunged forward and sank its fangs into my leg. I discovered right away that it's very hard to impress a gal with a dog hanging on your leg. I started screaming at the top of my lungs. She grabbed the dog, but it hung on for awhile before she could pull him off.

Luckily, my wounds weren't too severe. We patched them up and went out on our date anyway. As we were driving, I began to visualize how I could have handled the situation differently. If only I had stepped in the doorway with my left leg first, I could have convinced my date that I was the toughest guy around. The dog would have latched onto my artificial leg and I could have laughed in the face of the pain. "Go ahead," I could have said suavely, "Bite it again, sucker, I don't care." From that day forth, I've always entered strange places left leg first.

Second Serve

Our attitude is the window through which we see life's experiences. We can choose whether we see bright sunshine or a dirty window. Although there is much we cannot control in our lives, we can control the quality and content of our thoughts. I was unable to choose my hands or legs; however, I can choose my attitude.

Optimism or pessimism reflects one's expectations of what the future holds. The positive individual expects most things to work out for the best, while the negative thinker expects just the opposite. Our attitudes are a set of beliefs that predispose us to react to a person, place, or situation; therefore, belief systems are our choices. To remain optimistic, we must remind ourselves that we ultimately choose what we believe and what we think. How we think affects how we feel, and how we feel influences how we act. If you're having difficulty maintaining an optimistic attitude, focus on this thought: In life, we don't have reruns or instant replays—all we have is the *Today Show*.

To cultivate a more positive outlook, make this commitment: When you wake up every morning, think about what you have to look forward to during the upcoming day and remind yourself of the positive events in your past, rather than ruminating about negative past experiences. Make a deliberate effort to look for several activities you enjoy. Though we all have unpleasant tasks that need to be completed, if we closely examine our lives, we will find many positive things to do, think, and enjoy.

Chapter Twelve

Toward an Uncertain Future

I was getting anxious as my senior year at Loyola was drawing to a close. I realized that with graduation, I was going to face some big changes in my life. One of them involved tennis. I knew I was never going to play at Wimbledon or make my living on the pro circuit, yet for eight years the game had been one of the main focuses of my life. My self esteem had been largely built around my success as a tennis player and the acceptance it brought and now I was afraid my tennis career was coming to an end. Not only that, but I had enjoyed an insular lifestyle at Loyola where I knew almost everybody on the campus. Now I was faced with competing in the real world; with getting a job and with answering the question of what I was going to do with my life.

As the weeks went by in my final semester, I became increasingly depressed. Up to now I had always had clear-cut goals and objectives. In school, your goals are laid out for you; now I was going to have to establish my own agenda. I also knew that once school was over, I had to find a way to transfer the passion and commitment I felt for tennis to some other endeavor. But what? I didn't know.

I had chosen communications as a major because I enjoyed working with people and because television work seemed like a romantic and exciting field. Unfortunately, at the time I was in school, there were no television reporters with handicaps like mine, but the counselors and professors at Loyola encouraged me to pursue a career as an on-camera talent. A year later, Bree Walker, who has hands similar to mine, broke through and was hired as an anchorwoman in San Diego. But by that time, I had lost interest in television.

As I began to search for a career direction, I tried a number of things, some of them off-beat. For example, one of the first things I tried was stand-up comedy. I had always been able to make people laugh and I was able to get a gig at a local night club. I loved doing the routines and was received pretty well. It was fun, but I never took comedy seriously.

Something I always enjoyed at Loyola were my film classes. I produced and directed a movie for one class and I talked one of the tennis team members, Brad Todd, into helping me. Brad was tall, good-looking, and athletic. Throughout the film, the camera focused on him playing tennis. You saw him slam serves and return shots, but you never saw his opponent. As the movie progressed, Brad gradually began to miss shots (I was standing outside of camera range, throwing balls past him). He waved at overheads, dumped drop shots into the net and dove after passing shots that skipped by him in the corner. Finally, in frustration, he slammed his racket to the ground. The match ended, with him obviously the loser. The camera came tight on his face as he walked to the net to shake hands. The audience first saw the hand of the other player, then, as the camera panned back, they could see that the other player was in a wheelchair.

I thought it was a nifty film, it was judged best in its class by the Loyola communications department, but it marked both the beginning and the end of my movie-making career. If Rodney Dangerfield had nothing to worry about from my comedy career, neither did Steven Spielberg from my directing debut. I didn't know what I was looking for, I just knew I hadn't found it yet.

My father had given me the names of a few corporations with which he was familiar in Los Angeles and I managed to get a few interviews shortly before I graduated. I was offered a couple of sales positions with major companies, but I turned them down because they involved relocation out of California. I was turned down for a few positions. I don't know if my hands played a part in some of the rejections, although one time, indirectly, they did.

I had a problem whenever I would dress up to go to an interview. With only three fingers, I can't tie my own tie. Whenever I went to my job interviews, I had to get either my roommate or one of our neighbors to tie it for me. One day I was running late for an interview and I was horrified to find that nobody was in the apartment building. There was nobody around to tie my tie and I was running late for my interview. I tore down to the bus stop, my untied tie flapping in the breeze, and I climbed aboard a downtown bus. When I looked around, I found the only other person on the bus was a priest. I walked back to him and asked him if he could help me with my tie. He looked surprised.

"I've worn this collar so long I don't know if I remember how to do that," he said. Unfortunately, he wasn't kidding, he didn't remember. But with my verbal guidance he did the best he could. I thanked him and jumped off the bus and hustled up to the interview. The receptionist told me to go right into the office, but at the door I discovered the knot in my tie was still loose so I gave it a firm tug before marching into the office. The interview went smoothly, but when it was over I was told, "Don't call us, we'll call you."

I had to use the restroom on the way out and I froze when I saw myself in the mirror. The skinny part of my tie was dangling down below my belt and the fat part was only about six inches long. On top of that, the tie was all knotted up in a jumbled mess. No wonder I got the brush-off! That was the last time I ever asked somebody wearing a starched collar to tie my tie!

I talked to Brad Todd about my dilemma in finding a direction in my life. He had landed a position with a big eight accounting firm and had his career objectives in line. As we were speaking in his apartment, he reached to his bookshelf and handed me two books. The first book was *What Color Is Your Parachute* by Richard Bolles and the second was *The Power of Positive Thinking* by Dr. Norman Vincent Peale. Brad told

me the books had helped him a great deal and suggested I read them both. I did so and found Brad was
right — *What Color*... helped me focus on my strengths
and deal with my weaknesses. Dr. Peale's book taught
me some valuable principles and provided the inspiration I needed to pick myself back up.

Then one day I received a phone call from a representative of an urban Los Angeles high school. She
explained that she had seen articles about me in the
Los Angeles Times and asked if I would come by the
school and address some of the kids. I didn't have any
interviews that afternoon, so I said yes.

When I reached the school, I thought I had
entered a war zone. There were bars on the windows
and heavy gates around the outside. This was a tough,
inner-city school with all the accompanying problems of drugs, gangs, and truancy. I walked to the
gymnasium and was startled to see it was full of students. I met the lady I had spoken to on the phone
and told her I thought I was just going to be speaking
to one class.

"You are," she said. "This class just has 800 kids in
it."

I looked out to the audience and I felt like a
piece of steak that had just been thrown to the lions.
How was I, a short, suburban white kid going to relate
to this large audience of urban, black, restless
teenagers? I wasn't sure what was going to happen.

But something came over me when I began to
speak. Somehow, these kids were able to relate to my
experiences as a handicapped minority and in the
middle of my talk I saw a number of kids start to cry.
I may not have had a very smooth delivery, but what

I said came from the heart. I told the stories of my first dance, the time I was robbed, the trouble I had playing tennis and learning to write. I also told them about Garrett and how he was able to overcome some of his problems with a positive attitude. I told them that armed with the right outlook they could over-come the problems of their lives. I urged them to never let go of their dreams.

When I finished, the gymnasium was very quiet, then a groundswell of cheering and clapping welled up. Pretty soon, all the kids were on their feet. I was so stunned I just stood there frozen on the stage. Then a group of boys, all wearing the bandanas that signify gang members, leapt onto the stage and ran over to me.

"Mr. Crawford, if you ever find out who took your TV, you let us know," one of them said fiercely.

"Thanks, guys," I said in amazement. I shook their hands.

After things died down, the principal came over and said he thought I had a valuable message for teachers and administrators, as well as students. He said he was going to recommend me as a speaker to the other school districts in the area. I was delighted because for the first time in my life I had felt the same passion and the same drive as I had on the tennis court. I suddenly knew that this was what I wanted to do with my life. If I could get my message across to kids like this, I could talk to anybody. If I could make even a small difference in their lives, then all the things I had been through in my life would have been worth it. Suddenly, I was excited and looking forward to graduation and to my uncertain future.

ਟੇ

I moved back into my parents' house after graduation. I needed some time to explore my new career
direction and besides that, I didn't have a job or much
money. I expected life at home to be much like it was
before I left for Loyola, but it wasn't. I had grown used
to doing things my own way at college, but my parents' rules at home were as unyielding as ever. In
addition, my brother had gotten used to having the
run of the house without me around and we had
some conflicts.

I think it had been a relief for Brian when I went
away to college. He no longer had big brother's
accomplishments to live up to. In our case that was
especially difficult, because I received a lot of awards
and publicity for what I did in sports and although
Brian was a gifted athlete, he was "normal" and therefore didn't receive similar attention. To make matters
worse, when he did hit a home run, or make the all-
star team, the local newspapers referred to him as
"Brian Crawford, younger brother of Monte Vista
tennis star Roger Crawford." Because of me, the community expected big things of Brian in athletics and
he had some trouble playing under the pressure. Nat-
urally, he was resentful. As a result we often fought,
sometimes physically, but mostly verbally. We argued
over small things and called each other names,
although my handicap was off-limits. To his credit,
even during our fiercest fights, Brian never men-
tioned my hands or leg.

My brother has suffered because of my situation
and I think he still does. My parents were aware of the

problem and they worked hard to balance the attention I was getting from the community by acknowl-
edging even Brian's smallest accomplishments. I
sometimes felt they went overboard in Brian's favor,
which made me resentful. Now I know what a
difficult time they had trying to help us both. Brian
and I have never talked about our special relationship as brothers. But I love him very much and someday I hope we can.

He wasn't the only one having a tough time with
me in the house after college. Dad was still trying to
tell me what to do and I resisted his authority. I was
intimidated by him, though, and it was a cautious
rebellion. I would come home late at night and refuse
to take his advice, which he always gave freely. We
were polite on the surface, but underneath the ten-
sions simmered. One of our biggest disagreements
was over my career direction. Dad wanted me to find
a corporate job with benefits and job security,
whereas I was excited about becoming a speaker. Dad
wouldn't discuss the topic with me, he simply told me
what I should do. He was having trouble accepting
the fact that I was a man, capable of making my own
decisions. He and Mom had focused so much on
being the parents of a child with special needs that it
had become a major part of their identities. Reinforc-
ing that feeling was the fact that they were often singled out for parental advice by neighbors and the
media. By asserting my independence, I was forcing
them to make an uncomfortable change. At the same
time, Brian was about to leave home for college,
which meant for the first time in 20 years they were
going to be alone with each other. That caused more

anxiety because they had worked so hard at being good parents they had somewhat neglected their own relationship, though they are now slowly adjusting to their new roles.

People thought that teaching me to walk would be my parents' greatest task. Instead, the hardest thing for them has been to let Brian and me walk away.

A month after I returned from college Dad and I were avoiding each other in the house. Within a few weeks, I decided the only way out was to find a place of my own.

I searched for a couple of days and found an affordable apartment in Walnut Creek, a bedroom community about 20 miles east of San Francisco. On moving day, as I took my furniture and belongings out of the house, we both realized I was leaving home for good and the hard feelings began to melt away. I began to think back to all the times my parents had helped me out and how much I had depended upon them. When I broke my artificial leg, which happened several times each year as I got older and more involved with sports, Dad was the only one who could fix it. He had special tools manufactured specifically to work on my leg and he would sometimes spend hours putting the pieces back together. And I remembered Mom's peanut butter cookies and how I used to look forward to racing home after school with Donnie Ponzoni to eat them while they were still warm.

As we were collecting my things from the garage, Dad and I came across my old bicycle and it brightened our spirits. Dad had taught me to ride it when I was six years old. He made special straps on the handlebars so I could hang on like the other kids. One day, shortly after I learned to ride, I wobbled down the driveway into the street, right in front of an oncoming car. The car hit the bike and sent me flying. My artificial leg snapped off and bounced away down the street. Dad heard the collision and came running out of the house, while the driver, a teenage boy, jumped out of the car with a horrified look on his face. He had seen my leg fly off—he had no idea it was artificial.

"Oh no! Oh no!" the boy kept crying. Not only was my leg torn off, I had blood all over because I had scraped my hands on the pavement. Dad quickly sized up the situation. He could tell my cuts were superficial, so he calmly asked the boy where my leg was.

The teenage driver, looking sick, pointed to it. My shoe was still attached to the artificial foot. The boy looked at my leg and at me and slumped down on the car. He appeared ready to pass out.

Dad walked over and put his arm around the kid and told him about my artificial leg. After apologizing profusely, the relieved boy got back behind the wheel and lurched his car about three miles an hour down the block.

Shortly before moving out, I got a job teaching tennis at Crow Canyon Country Club in San Ramon under tennis pro Les Hansen. I was thrilled because Les was someone I greatly admired. Les was a role model for me—he was one of the nicest guys I'd ever met. He was tall, very good-looking, and had a way with the ladies at the club. He hired me to teach tennis and to work in the shop selling tennis equipment.

Luckily for me, Les also had a great sense of humor. One of my duties at the shop was to run the cash register. I told him that wouldn't be a problem, but the truth was, I had about as much luck operating the cash register as I had using a typewriter. My fingers were just too big to punch the right keys. Les used to kid me that the only reason he kept me on staff was because I charged people $20,000 for a tennis lesson.

We struck up a fast friendship that has lasted to this day. After work, we used to sit out by the courts and talk about tennis and about life. I think we both enjoyed these talks, gabbing as the sun set behind the smooth flanks of Mt. Diablo. Les was ten years older than I and he seemed to have been everywhere and done everything. He always encouraged me to follow my dreams, especially the two we often spoke about—getting my United States Professional Tennis Association (USPTA) certification and becoming a speaker. He had the ability to make my future seem exciting and limitless. There are certain moments in everybody's life that are recalled with a special fondness. Waxing philosophic with Les during those cool summer evenings is one of those times for me.

With Les's encouragement, I decided to try for my USPTA certification. I was very nervous about it because no handicapped player had ever won USPTA certification before. To become a certified professional, you have to pass both a written test and a playing test. The written test includes questions on tennis strategy, knowledge of the game, on tennis history, physiology, and on new teaching techniques. The playing test involved hitting shots for power and accuracy. Both tests are very stringent and require a great deal of concentration.

The USPTA holds its certification tests at random sites throughout the country, but as luck would have it, in 1985 it was held at Crow Canyon Country Club. That helped, but I knew the physical ability test was going to be tough because they test all parts of your game: various serves, volleys, forehands, backhands, spins, and a score of other playing skills. They rope off sections of the court and you have to hit your shots within small designated areas. There is a lot of pressure involved, but I had been practicing hard for these tests and I felt I was prepared.

On the day the tests were to be held, we all met in a conference room at the club. Several other players from northern California hoping to be certified were there and we had to stand and introduce ourselves. The room became quiet as a whisper when I stood up, and I could see that the entire certification team was looking right at my hands. After I sat down, the director of the team, John Weston, came over to me and said he needed to ask me a question.

"Part of the test is showing me how someone should correctly grip the racket," he said. "I'm hoping that won't be a problem for you because we have certain guidelines that we have to go by. We can't give any special consideration to anybody."

I told him I appreciated his concern and said I

wouldn't want it any other way. I wanted to make it on my own merits, or not at all.

The problem he foresaw, of course, was that I wouldn't be able to show students how to grip the racket because I couldn't grip it in the conventional ways myself. But, when it came to that part of the test, I took his hand and placed it on the racket to show him the western, eastern, and continental grips. I think he was relieved that I had solved the problem, but I still had to complete the rest of the two tests. I passed the written test without a problem, in part, I believe, because when I was learning to play, I had to think about virtually all parts of the game. Ironically, the written part often trips up the better, more natural players because they have never had to think about the techniques of their game as much as the rest of us.

During the playing test, we were required to hit a variety of shots with different grips. I had to explain to John Weston how I rolled the grip against my forearm to achieve the same type of spins and flat shots required from the different grips. He said as long as I could achieve the shots required, that's all that mattered. I appreciated John's straightforward approach. If I passed the tests, I wanted to feel I had done so under the same rules as everyone else. There were many players who didn't pass that day, but at the end of the afternoon my name was on the list of players who had become USPTA professionals. It remains one of my proudest accomplishments.

I played in a number of tournaments in California that year, often against some of the highest-ranked players in the country. There was prize money involved and it was during those tournaments that my lack of reach really began to tell. I was competitive with many of the players, but the better players, some of whom went on to play in the U.S. Open, Wimbledon and other USTA tournaments, could exploit my short reach. It was frustrating, but it underscored my desire to build a career outside tennis.

But at the same time, tennis continued to provide me with some of my most wonderful experiences. For example, I was invited to several celebrity tournaments around San Francisco. One of the greatest times I ever had was at a benefit tournament for the National Junior Tennis League, held by the San Francisco 49ers and the then Oakland Raider football teams. I played a doubles tournament with 49ers quarterback Joe Montana and we advanced past a number of teams, including one consisting of hard-hitting 49er safety, Ronnie Lott, and the Raiders huge defensive lineman, Howie Long. It was fun. The only problem was, these guys think tennis is a contact sport. The volleys at the net were murderous. When Ronnie and Howie rushed the net, they gave a new meaning to the word intimidation.

Joe and I got to play a final exhibition match against Bruno Yeager, the professional from the host club, Harbor Bay Isle, and the quarterback of the Raiders, Jim Plunkett. I was thrilled because Joe Montana and Jim Plunkett had always been my idols while I was growing up and now I was playing tennis with them! I could see why they were both world-class athletes. Although neither had played that much tennis, they were both hitting shots that usually only advanced players can hit, and although the match was played for a good cause and for fun, they were both very competitive. By the way, Joe and I won.

ॐ

Later that summer, I was asked to interview for the head coaching job of the San Ramon High School tennis team. San Ramon High had been our arch rival when I attended Monte Vista, but I really wanted to coach tennis and I assured the administration that the rivalry caused no problems for me. I got the job.

I was excited about coaching the team and the first day of practice I held a team meeting. I had all the players on the bleachers and I was introducing myself to them and giving them a pep talk about overcoming handicaps when a policeman walked up behind me.

"Excuse me, coach," he said. "But one of your players parked in the handicapped zone. He's going to have to move his car."

"What kind of car is it, officer?" I asked.

"It's a yellow Datsun," he said and I felt my face turn red.

It was my car. I had accidentally parked in the handicapped zone! (Although I'm allowed to park in handicapped zones because of my artificial leg, I rarely do.) The mistake put me in a tough spot—here I was telling my team to overcome their handicaps and I'm parked in the wheelchair zone! It was not my best moment as a coach, but the kids took it good naturedly and kidded me about it for several weeks.

Coaching the tennis team was one of the best

experiences I've ever had, but it was also one of the most challenging. I learned how to lead and teach young people, but I also learned what it was like to have to cut players from the team. Worst of all, I learned all about "little league parents."

Since only 12 guys could make the team and 32 tried out, I had to cut 20 players. That was very difficult for me because many of them had tried hard, but had little talent or experience. One player, who tried out, had a deformed hand. I was pulling for him, but I had to form the team according to who won the head-to-head competitions and he didn't make it. I took his defeat very hard. Having to cut him from the team kept me up a lot of nights. I asked him if he wanted to stay on the team as a manager, but he said no, he wanted to practice so he could make it next year. I put my arm around him and told him the same thing happened to me on the high school basketball team and encouraged him to keep playing. He later moved away from the school district, but I was very excited to hear that he made the team at his new school the following year.

Thankfully, in tennis, there were clear winners and losers and there weren't many judgement calls I had to make about who was going to make the team. But I did have to pair players for the doubles teams and that's where the trouble started. I began to get calls from parents almost every night, complaining about my doubles pairings. I was amazed at how serious the parents were about it. One father cursed so much that I told him if his son had talked that way, I would have thrown him off the team.

I also had a couple of players who displayed

abysmal manners on the court during our school matches. They would scream at their opponents and throw their rackets. Part of their behavior, I think, can be attributed to their emulation of the antics of the tennis professionals they saw on television—but it wasn't until I met the parents of these kids that I fully understood the origins of their negative attitudes. I put a stop to the temper tantrums and I told the players and their parents that anybody who wanted to play for me had to act like a gentleman, or they were off the team. As you can imagine, that didn't go over well with some of the parents, but I had one thing going for me that kept them in line. We were winners. In fact, we went undefeated in league play, including a victory over Monte Vista that decided the league championship.

If I grew a few new grey hairs during that season, I also learned a very important lesson. When you are at the top, whether you are leading a team, or a company, or a family, not every decision you make is going to be popular. No matter how successful you might be, you're not always going to make everybody happy. That was a sobering lesson for me because I always wanted to please everybody. I learned the hard way that to be a leader, you have to do what you think is right, then learn to live with the consequences.

As the school year waned and tennis season ended, I began to feel restless. I enjoyed teaching tennis at Crow Canyon, but found that being on my feet all day caused pressure sores on the stump of my leg. Also, I didn't have the passion for teaching as I did for playing. I told Tony Fisher that I was really anxious to see if I could establish a speaking career.

Tony told me that his wife, Micky, was a teacher at a local school and would probably be able to get me a speaking engagement there. About a week later, Micky called and asked if I could give a presentation at a school assembly. Although I had done it before, the thought of talking in front of so many people still made my knees shake. Surveys have shown that public speaking is the number one fear of people in the United States—death is number seven. (Bob Hope tells a story about a Christian who was about to be eaten by a lion in the Coliseum in ancient Rome. Just before he was devoured, the Christian whispered something in the lion's ear and the beast ran away and cowered in a corner. The emperor said he would let the Christian go free, but demanded to know what he told the lion. "I said he could eat me," said the Christian, "but afterwards he had to stand up and say a few words.")

Once my speech progressed, though, I relaxed and the words started to flow smoothly. I was amazed—it was similar to when I "hit the zone" in tennis. I realized that I could bring the same passion to speaking as I had to tennis!

Other school administrators heard about my presentation and I began to get other requests for speaking engagements. One of them included a school in Fresno, California, where I was to speak to an assembly of about 300 students. When I got there, the kids were quiet and well-behaved. I started out my speech with a joke; nobody laughed. The joke had always worked before, but these kids were as quiet as if they were in church. I recovered from the bombed joke and began to tell another story when all of a sudden the entire auditorium exploded in laughter. I looked around to see what was so funny, but I couldn't see anything so I kept on with my presentation. I told another joke and again the kids just sat there—I hadn't even raised a smile! Then, halfway into my next story, they all started laughing again.

Finally, I turned to the principal and asked him what was going on.

"Is the microphone working? Is there a delay in here?" I asked.

"Didn't you know?" he said. "These kids are deaf. Your speech is being signed to them, so they are getting your punchlines late."

This time it was my turn to laugh and from then on I waited until they could understand the signing before I went on. We all got a great chuckle from my misunderstanding.

A few weeks later, a friend talked me into going to hear Zig Ziglar, one of the top speakers in the nation. Ziglar, author of the best-selling book called *See You at the Top*, was speaking in San Francisco. I had never heard a professional speaker before and I was electrified by the effect he had on the audience. He was funny and charming, but more importantly, he talked about success in simple terms and made us feel we had the power to enhance our own lives. It was a boost for me to watch him work.

One evening, toward the end of the summer, I received a call from an executive with IBM in San Francisco. He told me that his son had been in the assembly at one of the schools where I had given my presentation.

"Roger," he said, "my son has come home for the

past 11 years and when I asked him what he did in school he has always said, 'nothing,' until today. Today, he gave me your speech, word for word. If you can do for my corporation what you've done for my son, I want you to come in."

After I gave my presentation at IBM, the boy's father told me that he had a number of people from other states who wanted to talk to me about giving presentations. When he said that, I knew that I was going to be doing some traveling . . . and maybe, maybe, this was going to work.

Second Serve

The velocity and complexity of our lives changes rapidly; therefore, today's success does not guarantee tomorrow's success. It is important not to let achievement replace original thinking or discourage risk taking.

To ensure competitiveness, we need to invest in our own growth and development. Over the years I've observed peak performers that make a habit of continual learning; one of my clients calls this "permanent homework." Sustained success requires this philosophy: I'll be better today than I was yesterday, but not as great as I'll be tomorrow.

Commit today to being a permanent student in life.

Chapter Thirteen

She Said "Yes"!

Although I had several good relationships with females while in high school and college, only a few took a romantic turn. Most ended up as friendships where I acted as a confidant and advisor. I enjoyed those friendships, but there was a nagging little voice in the back of my head that kept telling me the reason they hadn't proceeded farther was my handicap. As I got older, that nagging voice got louder and louder, until one night in Los Angeles it began screaming in my ear.

I was at a popular nightclub downtown when I was approached by an attractive lady, who asked me to dance. I took my hands out of my pockets to lead her to the dance floor; she looked at them and said, "Oh, too bad about your hands." And she just walked away. I tried to rationalize the situation—she was obviously immature and judged people by their exteriors. But deep down I was hurt. All my deepest fears about not being attractive to women were laid bare and I drew into myself for a few weeks to let the wound heal.

But sometimes good things happen when you least expect them. One day in the fall of 1984, I played a tennis match with my neighbor, Tim Dumas. Tim is a tall, sandy-haired, Southern gent, who lived in Louisiana before moving to Danville. Between matches we began talking about my speaking career. Tim had graduated from Louisiana Tech University in Ruston, Louisiana, and he suggested I contact a friend of his who hired speakers at the university. I did so, and my letter was turned over to the new student program director at the school, Donna Shankles.

Donna reviewed my brochure and said in a letter that she would be interested in having me speak and we began to work out the details. I called her on the phone and was so intrigued by her Southern accent and her friendly manner, I raced over to Tim's house and looked up her picture in his university yearbook. I couldn't believe my luck! She was very attractive and had a wonderful, warm smile.

On January 28, 1985, I flew to Monroe, about 30 miles from Ruston, and met Donna at the airport. She wore a dark blue skirt with a plaid jacket and she waved as I walked into the terminal. I was looking forward to some of the famous Southern hospitality I had heard so much about. I wasn't disappointed. Donna and I hit if off immediately and we talked nonstop through dinner.

I was impressed by her zest and enthusiasm for life and the more we talked the more I began to feel she was the kind of person who could look past my handicap to see me as a person. She possessed a lot of self confidence and she wasn't afraid to ask me questions about my hands or my leg. I liked that because talking about them made us both feel more comfortable.

After dinner we drove to a small bed-and-breakfast where Donna had reserved a room for me. We sat on a couch in the lobby of the inn and talked some more . . . she told me about her future plans of graduating and starting her own business. I was impressed by her focus and maturity. After she left, I sat in my room and watched the moon come up. I knew if I wasn't careful I was going to fall in love with this Southern belle.

Despite the fact that Donna had done TV and radio ads and had put up posters all over the campus, the audience at my presentation was smaller than we expected. The problem was there was a championship basketball game going on at the same time. I wasn't concerned about the rest of the audience because during my speech Donna sat in the front row. She laughed at all my jokes and she cried at the touching parts, so I considered my presentation a great success.

Donna was very disappointed by the small turnout, though, and I did my best to cheer her up. We had a wonderful evening together and I wasn't looking forward to leaving. Then a terrific thing happened on the way to the airport. A huge fog bank rolled in—a rarity in northern Louisiana—and the airport closed down. I was never so glad to see fog in my life!

Donna had expressed a desire to visit San Francisco during our talk over dinner and this gave me more time to talk her into it. (The fog was the perfect backdrop!) She called her parents and they insisted on putting me up in their home. We had a lot of fun that evening and it was clear we had formed the beginning of a strong friendship. Of course, later that night when Donna and I bumped into each other in the hall — she had just taken a shower and was wearing only her father's shirt — I entertained thoughts that exceeded mere friendship. But Donna was a very popular gal on campus and she was dating a number of different guys.

In a way, that turned out to be a positive thing, because I was forced to put a check on my feelings for her. As time went on and we continued our relationship over the phone, I figured the best I could do was to be her friend and so we talked openly and honestly about everything. When you begin a relationship with somebody you think is "The One" there is often a tendency to try to cover up weaknesses and to try to impress.

I had never before talked to a woman about what it felt like to have a handicap. Being open with Donna was a big step for me because it meant I had gained enough self confidence to put my trust in another person.

It was still early in our relationship when she came to visit me in California. She was excited to see the sights of San Francisco and I took her to every romantic place I could think of — we listened to the minstrels in Golden Gate Park, rode the cable cars, explored Fisherman's Wharf and Chinatown, and we toured the Monterey Peninsula and the Napa Wine Country.

As I was planning the Wine Country trip, I wondered if there would be a situation where Donna would touch my hands. I thought back to when I was a young boy and my mom would hold my hand as we walked. Whenever anybody would pass by, I would pull my hand away and put it in my pocket because I thought she would be ashamed of being seen holding my hand. Then one time, someone walked by and Mom held my hand tight and wouldn't let me pull away. I asked her "Do you think there will ever be a time when somebody else will want to hold my hand the way you do?"

"Someone will hold your hand if you put a smile on your face, take your hands out of your pockets, and show that you are proud of who you are," she said.

I remembered that advice when Donna arrived at the airport. Later in the day we were in my tiny apartment in Walnut Creek and I took my hands out of my pockets and put my right hand on Donna's knee. Donna reached over and grasped my hand and she smiled at me. We began talking about my hands. She wanted to know all about what the surgeons had done and the medical background on the birth defect. She was very sensitive, yet she was also very curious. I knew from that moment on that our relationship was going to grow.

Donna came to visit me during her school breaks and holidays and, in between, our phone bills rivaled the national debt. Although we became closer, I could sense she was still holding back from becoming seriously involved. I thought it was because of my hands. I assumed she was apprehensive about marrying someone with such a handicap.

The first serious disagreement we had was when I finally asked her to make a commitment to our relationship. We had a long talk and she admitted that my hands were an issue for her. When she was growing up, she hadn't envisioned that the man she would marry would be handicapped. But my hands were only part of the problem. She was also concerned about getting her degree in fashion merchandising and pursuing her own career in Louisiana. She had set some very clear goals for herself and moving to California would have thrown her off course.

At the end of our talk, she made a decision.

"I think it's best that we stop seeing each other," she said. Then she added a line that I had heard before.

"I want to be your friend," she said. "And I want you to know that I think the person you marry is going to be so lucky—but at this point, I'm not ready to make a commitment."

Despite all the other things she had said, I was convinced that the only problem between us was my handicap. I know now that isn't true, but at the time I figured I had to face facts—I wasn't anybody's version of "Mr. Right." I hung up the phone and fell apart. The love of my life just wanted to be my friend when I had already picked out names for our children!

Later that night I had dinner with my parents and told them about Donna's decision. Dad, as usual, had some good advice. "One thing you should do right now is work on Roger Crawford," he said. "Focus on improving yourself and getting on with your life." While I was grateful for Dad's words, I knew it wasn't going to be easy. This was something I had to work out by myself.

I felt like calling Donna and begging her to come back, but I knew I had to have the strength to let her make her own decision. I didn't call or write her for several weeks. Although I thought about her every day and hoped she would change her mind, I began to feel I could live with the consequences if she didn't. I realized I wasn't afraid to be by myself. Then one cold December night when I was on the road in New Jersey, I called home to get my phone messages. To my surprise, there was one from Donna. She wanted me to call. I did, right away. We talked small talk for awhile, then she said something to me that I'll always remember the way you remember the words to a beautiful song.

"Roger, I've made a mistake," Donna said. "We had something special and I just didn't realize it. Your heart is much more important than your hands. There isn't any reason we can't follow our dreams together."

I proposed to Donna that spring during a trip we took to Disney World in Florida. I was so nervous that night I drove right through an interstate toll booth without paying. When the highway patrol pulled us over about ten miles down the road, nobody was more surprised than me. I was so distracted I hadn't even noticed the toll booth! I had something more important on my mind. That night, on bended knee, I asked Donna to marry me and she said "Yes!"

I was ecstatic for weeks, but one thought was troubling me. I felt deprived that I would never be able to wear a wedding ring. I was jealous of people who could wear them, and when I attended Tim Dumas' wedding shortly before my own, I felt sharp pangs of envy when Tim's wife put the wedding ring on his finger. I shared my feelings with Donna and she told me not to worry. A few days later she gave me a gold neck chain similar to a necklace she always wore. "Think of it as a wedding ring, only a little larger," she said.

A few weeks prior to the marriage ceremony a new worry popped into my head. Since I couldn't wear a ring, how was Donna going to place the wedding ring on my finger during the ceremony? And how were we going to get married if Donna couldn't slip a ring on my finger? I had never heard of a wedding without wedding rings. When I finally expressed my fears to our minister, he just laughed.

"I'll just perform a one-ring service," he said.

I breathed a huge sigh of relief. I hadn't even known there was such a thing as a one-ring service, but it sure sounded like a good idea at that point. After all Donna and I had been through to get here, I didn't want our marriage derailed for lack of a ring finger!

The wedding ceremony was held July 26, 1986, at the Trinity United Methodist Church in Ruston. It was a warm day, with the temperature hovering around 100 degrees. Surprisingly, I had very few butterflies in my stomach before the ceremony. I knew we were making the right decision. Before the ceremony, my father, brother, Ray, and Ron, sat and reminisced about old times. Some of the stories were so funny that tears were running down our faces.

Finally, the wedding march began. The music welled up out of a huge pipe organ behind us. When I glanced back at the organ I saw Donna's reflection. I turned around and saw her walking arm and arm with her father. She was lovely. They walked up the aisle past my parents, who were crying. Seeing them caused a sudden pain in my stomach. I wanted to run to them and reassure them they hadn't lost a son — but of course, in a way they had. I was changing my family and they no longer were at the head of that family. As Donna reached my side, though, I knew this was the natural order of things — there is usually a little pain with any real growth. The ceremony went smoothly and Donna helped me put her ring on her finger. It was my most fulfilling moment.

We honeymooned in Hawaii and spent a lot of time on the beach. Since Donna didn't like to get in the surf, she stayed behind and guarded my leg while I snorkled. I loved watching the tropical fish darting around and I saw a number of other snorklers swimming nearby. I noticed many of them weren't looking at the fish, they were watching me swim. I've always loved an audience so I started diving down and doing underwater flips. Pretty soon I was as big an attraction as the fish!

On more than one occasion I've had friends express the idea that because I've dealt with my handicap and I've found someone who has accepted me for what I am on the inside, that everything else must be easy in our marriage. That's not true. Donna and I have disagreements just like everybody else, but regardless of what we may argue about, our relationship remains based on mutual respect and trust.

The first time we went to bed together I had to put my total trust in Donna's hands because I had to take my leg off in front of her. To a person with an artificial limb, taking it off in front of another person who isn't used to it is often the hardest thing to do.

Donna and I sat on the bed and without looking at her I pulled off my leg and jumped immediately under the covers. Donna smiled and put her hand on my leg. We talked for a few minutes, then I slowly pulled my leg out and she gently stroked it. Somehow, that gesture was as intimate and touching as the act of love itself.

&

One of my greatest fears during our courtship was how Donna's parents, Donald and Mary Shankles, and her sister, Sherri, were going to feel about me. What would they think about having a handicapped person marrying Donna? That question weighed heavily on my mind because I wasn't sure at all how they would react to me being something more than just Donna's friend. At the time Donna and I met, I was just starting my speaking career and was struggling financially. I knew my money and my hands weren't going to impress her folks. I just said a little prayer and hoped for the best.

But once I got to know Mary, who owns a successful real estate office in Ruston, and Donald, an insurance executive in nearby Jonesboro, I knew I had nothing to worry about. Sherri is also a very friendly, open-minded, and intelligent person, and all three accepted me with open arms. Not all families would have been so understanding.

I also worried about Donna's friends. Donna had always dated handsome men and her girlfriends are all attractive and have good-looking husbands and boyfriends. How was she going to explain me to them? It helped that I had spoken at Louisiana Tech because most of her friends had been in the audience (in fact, they may have *been* the audience) and already knew about my hands and leg. However, I'm sure it took time for some of them to get used to the way I look.

Others, however, haven't always been so understanding. For example, at a party Donna once overheard a couple discussing our relationship. A young lady was saying, "I can't understand why Donna would want to marry Roger. Does he have a lot of money?"

The comment hurt Donna very much, but I'm sure there are people who often wonder similar things. It's hard for them to understand that an able-bodied person can love and marry someone who's physically challenged. To those people, I can only say "You can see my handicap. I can't see yours. We all have them."

One thing that Donna and I have had to work out was my inability to do a lot of things that have traditionally been looked at as "a man's job." For example, I can't hammer nails. As a result, Donna has had to become a good carpenter. However, it took her awhile to get used to the idea of being the only one that could do those tasks.

In a lot of ways we've had to reverse the traditional roles around the house. Donna has to do a lot of things like opening stubborn jar lids and I help with the dishes and cleaning the house. Having me handle the dishes made Donna a nervous wreck at first, especially when she came home one day to find me washing her finest china. But so far, I have yet to break a single piece.

Unfortunately, my record with the lawn mower isn't quite as good. Our present home has a small lawn and I bought a lawn mower when we moved. I bought the type you have to yank on a rope handle to start. I brought it home and happily pushed it out onto the driveway so I could start it and mow our lawn. After a half hour of pulling on the starter cord I began to think that the mower I'd bought was devised by some sadist who wanted to wreak his twisted revenge on the world. Finally, I asked Donna to help me, but I made her start the machine inside the garage where the neighbors couldn't see us. That way I could come out with the engine roaring.

After a few months of wrestling with the monster, I finally got the hang of it and now I can usually start it up right away. Of course, the new mowers come equipped with electronic ignitions and start with a push of a button!

Although I emphasize the importance of maintaining a positive outlook on life in my presentations, I don't always have good days. I recall one day when my microphone went off during my speech, I missed two flights back to San Francisco International and when I finally arrived, my luggage was missing. Donna picked me up and on the way home, we immediately got stuck in a traffic jam. I started complaining loudly and finally Donna said: "Roger, there's something you need to listen to."

She opened the glove compartment, pulled out a cassette tape, and plugged it in.

I heard a voice say, "I'd rather have one leg and a positive attitude than two legs and a negative attitude."

It was my own tape.

I looked at her and we both laughed.

People frequently ask Donna and me if we plan to have children. We can't wait. Some birth defects involving hands and feet are hereditary, but doctors don't know for sure that my handicap can be passed on to our children. We also do not know that it cannot. There is no guarantee that our baby will be perfect, but is there for any couple, for any child? Even the most able-bodied couples face an uncertain risk when they have children. It's a risk we all share.

At first, Donna and I talked about adopting a child. We weren't sure how we would feel about having a child that looked like me. But then, I asked myself, where would I be if my parents had thought that way. At the same time, we would prefer an able-bodied child.

I have a lot of fears, though, even if the child is normal. I often wonder how my own children will react to me. I've talked to handicapped parents of normal children and they say the children never even noticed the handicaps—they figured everybody's parents were handicapped. I know that there are some things, such as putting together models or puzzles, that I won't be able to do with them. That makes me nervous because I'm concerned that the other kids will tease my children about me. I also get concerned when I go to places like the public swimming pool and watch all the parents teaching their children to swim. In order to do that, the parents stand on the bottom of the pool, something I can't do.

I'm more concerned, though, about how I will react if our child is born with physical problems. I'm afraid for two reasons. First, I'm afraid for the child because I know exactly what he or she will have to go through. People are often surprised when I admit my fear because they assume since I've been through it, I could help a child deal with having a physical limitation. However, I know there is no way I could shield the child from the pain of being born different—if I did, the child would end up like Tommy, living an unproductive life with a wall between him and the world.

Second, I'm afraid for myself. Watching the child grow would cause me to have to relive the painful experiences of my own childhood, especially those difficult adolescent times.

Despite these limitations, though, I feel confident I can be a good father. I think the most important things you share with your child are the examples you set in your own life. I hope I can show my children how to deal positively with obstacles they will face.

Donna always says that nothing would mean more to her than to have a child who looks like me and has ten fingers and ten toes. Yet, even if we knew our child were to be born with handicaps similar to mine, we would still be eager parents—because although in some ways life may be tougher for somebody with three fingers and one leg, there is still a world of opportunity out there for a person with a can-do attitude.

Second Serve

When my precious daughter, Alexa, was born I wondered how she would react when she realized I was somewhat different from the other dads in the neighborhood. Surprisingly, my daughter has taught me a great deal about unconditional love.

Often, children of blind or deaf parents become their mother's or father's eyes or ears. In certain situations, Alexa has had to be my hands. She takes great pride in assisting me with tasks that prove difficult; for example, opening juice pouches. You may be familiar with these torture devices designed for aggravation. (You see, they are constructed to survive the abuse of a school lunch box.) The plastic wrapping around the straw is like armor that refuses removal. After you finally strip it off, your job is then to squeeze the juice container until it is about to burst, and then strategically spear the tiny straw through an even tinier opening to access the juice. Any miscalculation or overaggressiveness will send a shower of juice everywhere—usually resulting in a direct hit in the eye! My accomplishing this task requires some creativity. I place the box between my knees, compress it until is about to explode, then, with the straw grasped with my two hands, I attack.

After watching this fiasco several times, Alexa has decided that the juice box is now her responsibility. She is delighted with her own dexterity and says proudly, "That's my job, Daddy!"

Chapter Fourteen

The Power of Prayer

During my travels around the country, a lot of people ask me how I made my peace with God. There were times when I was younger when I would grow very bitter about God for allowing me to be born with a handicap. In my silent prayers I would ask, "Why did you do this to me? Why do I have this kind of burden?" I spent many angry and tearful nights asking these questions, wondering why God had seen fit to punish me even before I was born.

As I learned more about God and life, and I read the Bible more thoroughly, I began to believe that He had created special roles for all of us and that He had a special plan for me, too. Maybe there was a reason I was born the way I was. It helped that I had gained some success through tennis and in other areas of my life because I began to understand that although He had made me different, He had also given me special gifts.

I began to pay close attention to the lessons of the Bible about thinking positively and taking the gifts that you have been blessed with, and using them to the best of your ability. I was struck by the strength of these teachings and how empowering faith and prayer can be.

As I got older, I began to believe more strongly that God gave me my hands and leg for a reason. Part of that reason, I believe, is that it has led me to my speaking career. Being able to speak in front of thousands of people about the power of positive thoughts and actions — and hopefully helping some people to have a fuller and happier experience in life — is perhaps part of His master plan for me.

One experience I had that helped me understand this took place after one of my presentations. A pregnant lady came up to me and wanted to talk. She told me that a friend had taken her to hear me speak and she said my message had meant a great deal to her. I thanked her and told her I hoped everything would go well during her delivery of the baby. She asked me for my address, then she began to cry. She left soon after that, but about two weeks later I received a letter from her. It read

"Dear Roger; I was in your audience and I talked to you two weeks ago. I'm the woman who was going to have a child. I just wanted to let you know that my child has two fingers on both of his hands. I found that out through a sonogram three days before I went to hear you speak. I wanted you to know that I was in despair about my child's condition until I heard what you had to say. Now I know there is hope for my child and that with some positive thoughts, actions, and prayers, I can help my child live a fulfilling life. I want to thank you from the bottom of my heart for making such a difference."

Her letter had a great impact on me. It gave me a greater sense of purpose and a greater understanding of how I might use the gifts I was given. It also helped me understand that without my handicap, I doubtlessly would not have chosen a speaking career. If I still harbored any of the questions and doubts about God's benevolence, they completely disappeared. My faith is now strong.

I believe that for every obstacle God puts in our way there is also an opportunity. The power of faith and the power of prayer can help overcome these obstacles and let us see the opportunities more clearly. I know that relying on God's judgment and believing in the good in life have gotten me through some tough times.

Although Donna and I each have our own individual relationship with God, our mutual faith is an important part of our own relationship. We often pray together, in church, at the dinner table, or wherever we happen to be when we feel like praying. Whenever a problem arises between us, Donna and I turn to God for guidance. I believe God put Donna in my life for a reason, not only to share my love, but to be my partner in all phases of my life, including at home and in our work.

One of my favorite prayers is the Serenity Prayer. I often say it to myself when things aren't going well or when I have a big decision to make. "God grant me the serenity to accept the things I cannot change, give me the courage to change what I can, and give me the wisdom to know the difference."

One of my favorite spiritual leaders is Dr. Robert

Schuller, who is the minister of the Crystal Cathedral in Garden Grove, California. His weekly television show, "Hour of Power," has been a constant source of inspiration to me. I share many of his beliefs. He is a strong advocate of combining spiritual goals with good common sense and his message stresses the importance of developing a good attitude and high self esteem. He also knows what it's like to face life with a physical handicap; his daughter lost her leg in a motorcycle accident.

One of my dreams had been to be on his program. In 1989 that dream came true. He invited me to be a guest on the "Hour of Power" television show. The Crystal Cathedral is an incredible structure. It is made almost entirely of glass and when the sunlight slants through, a natural rainbow spreads throughout the interior. I was awed just being in the cathedral, let alone being asked on the show and to address the congregation.

The taping of the show went off without a hitch and the producer said it would air in April 1989. I was looking forward to it, but at the last moment they called me and told me I had been rescheduled to a later date. I was disappointed at the delay until they told me who it was that preempted me...it was Mother Teresa! She had given Dr. Schuller a surprise interview and he wanted to air it right away. I can't think of anybody I'd rather have preempt me.

Chapter Fifteen

The Truth Ain't Hard to Remember

By the end of 1985, my speaking career had gotten off to a good start and I was touring around the country, talking to a variety of corporations, universities, associations, and youth. I received a lot of satisfaction from my work because presenting the empowering and overriding importance of high self esteem and a positive outlook on life was a way for me to give something back to my community and to my country.

When I first began to speak, I would begin my talk holding my notes and standing behind a lectern. But after a few months, I found that every time I told an audience I have an artificial leg, they would all crane their necks to look around the lectern to see it. Slowly I gained enough confidence to come out from behind the speaker's stand and to stop using notes. The career was still new to me and early in 1986 I was still having difficulty preparing my remarks and deciding how to enhance my message. It was during this time that I met John Savage, a life insurance executive from Toledo, Ohio. I was in San Jose, California, speaking to the San Jose Life Underwriter's Association, and John was also there to address the audience. John was an old pro whom I greatly admired. He had a loving wife and family and was very successful in his business career. He took great care of himself physically and I knew he had a rich spiritual life. John is world renowned in his field and he is also one of the friendliest people I've ever known. I went to him for some advice on how to prepare my speech. I told him I was having trouble determining which stories I should tell and which principles I should share.

We were sitting in an empty auditorium and John was a row in front of me.

"How do you know what's right?" I asked him.

He looked at me and said, "Roger, if you want to be a great speaker, if you want to be a great communicator, you only have to know one thing."

Then he reached back, grabbed my tie and pulled my face close to his. "Roger," he said. "The truth ain't hard to remember."

If you've ever been to San Francisco and watched the summer sun cut right through the Pacific fog to reveal a crystal clear blue sky day, then you have an idea of what John Savage's words meant to me. I had been wracking my brain trying to come up with just the right anecdotes and messages when the answer was right in front of me all the time. The Truth. It's simple, it's effective, and it works wonders.

It was a real turning point for me. Suddenly my focus was clear. Now, when I look out in the audience, if I see someone with a tear in their eye, or a great big smile on their face and if I can't cry or laugh with that audience member, if I can't feel the story as much as they are feeling it, then I know that I have to rethink what I am saying and ask myself "What is the truth?" Am I telling the truth as I know it? Whenever I have trouble developing my presentation, I always recall John Savage's words.

❧

Sometimes truth, or wisdom, can be found in unlikely places. A few years ago I had just finished speaking in Vancouver, British Columbia, and I was driving south to Seattle for another engagement. At the United States–Canada border, I was stopped by a Canadian patrolman. We talked casually and during the conversation he asked me three questions: Where have you been? How long have you been there? Where are you going? They were simple enough questions, but as I was driving away I was struck by how profound they really are. I've found these are great questions to ask myself whenever I'm feeling a little lost or confused. If I can answer them, I know I'm back on course.

People often ask me what it's like traveling 150 to 200 days a year. I say that it can be wearisome, but there are a lot of advantages to staying in so many hotel rooms. My wife and I haven't bought a bar of soap since 1986, we have 15,000 bottles of shampoo, and a number of sewing kits. Seriously, we enjoy the travel, although it certainly can have its moments.

A common thing on airplanes is the misconception many flight attendants have about my hands.

Whenever I ask for a beverage, most of them look skeptically at my hands. Then they place the plastic cup carefully between my fingers . . . and they don't let go! They don't believe I can hang onto it. I literally have to yank the cup out of their hands. I've been in situations where they've asked me four or five times whether I have a grasp on the cup before they reluctantly let go.

One of the most touching experiences I've had during my travels occurred after I gave a presentation in New Jersey to a teacher in-service group.

Although the education system in America has taken some hard knocks lately, I've always enjoyed addressing educators. I think teachers and administrators are doing one of the most important jobs in the country. They have the wonderful opportunity not only to touch lives, but to change lives, every single day. Unfortunately, I believe educators aren't as appreciated as they should be in our society, especially given that they are the guardians of our future. Many teachers play a major part in their students' lives—I remember how much Mr. Cross and Mrs. MacMillan meant to me when I was growing up—and I feel it's an honor to be able to talk to them.

After my talk in New Jersey, a young teacher came up to me and asked me to visit her classroom. She was a special education teacher. I met her the following morning at her school in Vernon, New Jersey. We walked into her classroom and I remember seeing a number of quotes written on her chalkboard. One, by Albert Schweitzer, said, "The greatest discovery a human being can make is that he can change his life by changing his attitude."

There were also quotes from Benjamin Franklin, Abraham Lincoln, Norman Vincent Peale, and other famous Americans. The last quote said, "I would rather have one leg and a positive attitude than two legs and a negative attitude." It was from me! I laughed and told her that I was flattered to have made the chalkboard with such illustrious company.

I met a few of her students. Their problems ranged from severe physical handicaps to learning disabilities. One boy, Bobby, had cerebral palsy. He was in a wheelchair and he had lost the use of his arms and legs. He couldn't speak or control the saliva from his mouth, which ran down his face onto a bib he had to wear around his neck. I had come in contact with a number of physically challenged people in my life and I thought that I would be able to look at anyone who had a disability and be able to handle it. I didn't think I'd see anything that would make me feel uncomfortable or tight in my stomach. But seeing Bobby did. When I saw the saliva running down his face and his lifeless arms and legs, I almost cried.

It was an awkward situation because I didn't know how he communicated and suddenly I realized very clearly how some people feel when they meet me for the first time. I smiled at Bobby, told him it was very nice to meet him and I put my hand on his shoulder. Suddenly he started to wiggle his head back and forth. I looked at his teacher, and she smiled.

"He wants to tell you something," she said.

She unzipped his backpack on the back of his wheelchair and pulled out something that looked like a halo. A long plastic stick came out the top of the halo, like an antenna. She placed the halo on Bobby's head and plugged in a small, laptop computer on the front of his wheelchair. Bobby bent his neck and began typing on the computer, using the long stick to push the keys.

"Roger, look over Bobby's right shoulder," the teacher said.

I watched as Bobby typed a message that came up on the small computer screen.

It said, "Dear Mr. Crawford, I really like your quote, 'You can see my handicap, but I can't see yours.'"

Bobby paused for a moment, then typed in capital letters, "I ALSO HAVE A POSITIVE ATTITUDE."

Anytime I get a little discouraged or down, I think back to Bobby. Bobby isn't the only winner in that story. The effort that his teacher had put forth to establish a relationship with each one of these special children is, to me, a shining example of how good human beings can be.

Not everything has gone smoothly during my presentations. Once, I was speaking on the East Coast to a group of about 1000 high school students in the school gymnasium. Just before I gave my presentation, the activities director told me the acoustics in the gym were very good and I wouldn't need a microphone. I gazed around and it looked just like any other gym to me and I asked him what made the acoustics so good. Just before I was to talk, he admitted the public address system was broken. I told him I couldn't shout out my speech and I asked if there was anything he could do. He thought for a moment, then said he would be right back. As I was walking up to the lectern, he came back with a bullhorn he had borrowed from the football coach. The bullhorn was oversized and had a blinking red light on the top.

I gave my entire speech through that bullhorn with the light flashing the entire time. The students loved it. I think they had some empathy for me because they could see I was struggling to hold up the bullhorn. I had to hold it with both hands and by the end of the speech my arms felt like they were going to fall off.

Another time things got a little crazy on the road was during a trip Donna and I took to Charlotte, North Carolina. I was going to speak to a group of 27,000 people, the largest group I had ever addressed. I was nervous and a little on edge when we landed at the airport. When we arrived, a driver who worked for the association I was to address picked us up and drove us to the Sheraton Hotel. When we checked in, I could hear our driver arguing with the hotel clerk.

"I know there is a reservation for Mr. and Mrs. Crawford, please check again," he was saying.

Finally, the matter was resolved and the bellboy took our bags to our room.

The driver told us to expect a present for each of us and a large basket of fruit, courtesy of the hotel management. He also said the business card of my association contact would be attached to the fruit basket. My contact was going to meet us for dinner at 7 P.M.

Donna and I thanked him and went up to our room. We went in and there was no present, no fruit basket, and no business card.

"Sloppy management," I thought to myself.

After we showered and cleaned up, we called the hotel manager, who was very apologetic about the missing fruit and presents. Within 10 minutes a huge, beautiful basket of fruit and flowers arrived with a couple of nice presents: perfume and shaving equipment.

There was still no business card, but we got ready for dinner and went to the lobby just before 7 o'clock. We waited until almost 7:30 P.M. and we began to get a little uneasy when I was paged to the front desk.

"Mr. Crawford, there is a phone call for you."

I took the call.

"Roger?" It was the host who had sent the driver for me at the airport. "Guess what? The driver took you to the wrong hotel."

I put the phone down and laughed so hard Donna came over to see what was the matter. When I told her, she starting laughing, too. After all the fuss we had made over the missing reservations, the fruit and the presents, we weren't even in the right hotel! Even the manager laughed over the situation and he invited us to stay as long as we wished. After being treated so well at the Sheraton — even without reservations — it has become one of our favorite hotels and we always make a point of staying over when we are in the area.

ॐ

During my travels around the country, I am usually greeted at the airport or the hotel by the meeting planner of the corporation or association who has invited me to speak. I always laugh when they tell me they brought a picture along so they could make sure they recognized me.

One day, not long ago, I was speaking in front of

a group of executives in San Francisco. I met the host of the program, and I asked him if he was all squared away on the information he needed from me to do my introduction. One of the greatest fears any speaker has is that his or her introduction will out-shine the speech, so I wanted to get an idea of what he was going to say.

He said to me, "Roger, I've had quite a lot of inter-national experience speaking in front of groups and I really don't think I need a prepared introduction. If you don't mind, I'd like to do an impromptu intro-duction, I feel it adds a lot of flavor."

I told him I didn't mind at all and waited as the program began.

Our host began his introduction with some of my background.

"Roger Crawford has had some successes in his life, but he was born with a physical handicap," he told the audience of corporate executives. "I couldn't help but notice as I was talking to Roger that he was born with . . . three legs."

A hush fell over the audience, but the host didn't notice his faux pas. Of course, he meant to say three fingers. As it turned out, it was perhaps the most elec-trifying introduction I've ever had. If anybody in that audience wasn't paying attention before, they cer-tainly were after that. Everybody was wide-eyed trying to see this guy with three legs.

Once, when I was speaking at a school in Florida, my audience was the support staff of an entire school district—the teachers, secretaries, custodians, food servers, and administrators. My talk was about how important their jobs are in the society and how they can make a tremendous difference in the lives of so many children.

After I was finished with my presentation, a lady in an apron came up to me and gave me a big hug. I could tell the students were served lasagna that day because it was all over her apron and now it was all over my suit. I didn't care, though, because the lady was so excited she had tears in her eyes.

"That was the most wonderful speech I've ever heard," she gushed. Then she hugged me again. "You know what I do? I serve hot lunches to the kids. I don't have very much education and I never thought I could make a difference. But when you talked about building a positive attitude, and when you said: 'If you see a child without a smile give em' one of yours', and 'Never pass up an opportunity to catch someone doing something right'... well, you were talking right to me.

"Now, when a youngster comes through my line, I'm going to say something to brighten their day. The only thing I'm scared about is that I work at a very rough high school. There's a lot of problems there, a lot of drugs and a lot of kids coming from broken homes. They might think I'm silly and laugh at me."

I put my arm around her.

"I don't think they will," I told her. "Because I'm sure the only smile a lot of those kids will see all day is going to be yours."

Three weeks later I received a letter, carefully written in longhand.

"Dear Roger. I'm the one who came up to you

and got lasagna on your suit. I just wanted to thank you for the speech you gave. I tried the things you suggested, even though I was worried the kids were going to laugh at me. Every time I saw a student at school, I said something positive and I smiled. I want to tell you what happened."

In the letter, she had drawn a diagram that showed two identical lines of food, like a smorgasbord. She explained that the kids could go down either line since the food was the same on each side.

"I sit there and scoop up the lasagna, or the spaghetti, or whatever we're serving that day and I do it with a smile and I say something nice. Mr. Crawford, now I have a problem. All the kids line up in my line. My line is always twice as long as the other line."

I often carry her letter around with me because when the plane is late, or I'm stuck in a traffic jam somewhere far from home and I start wondering if this is really what I want to do with my life, I take it out and read it. It never fails to cheer me up... or make me hungry for lasagna.

Second Serve

have many scars that are visible, but throughout my life I've realized that the *invisible* scars—such as low self-esteem, negative attitudes, and lack of will—are much more difficult to overcome. My valued friend Dr. Robert Schuller says, "Faith can turn your scars into stars." I, too, believe that you can counteract your fearful emotions with a statement of faith. My favorite faith strengthener is Philippians 4:13: "I can do all things through Christ, who strengthens me." Remember, discouragement is a choice.

Hope is wishing; faith is believing. When you begin to lose faith, remember that you were made by God. He created you. When I look at my hands, I'm reminded that God doesn't make mistakes. See yourself as God sees you—valuable, special, and worthy of happiness.

Chapter Sixteen

Miss Liberty

A few years ago Donna and I were in New York and we visited the Statue of Liberty. I was really excited about seeing Lady Liberty because she is a perfect symbol to the world that the citizens of the United States welcome all peoples — regardless of their beliefs, or what they look like. She represents the values of tolerance, freedom, and understanding.

The day was clear and bright when Donna and I reached Liberty Island. The day was so nice, in fact, that hundreds of other tourists were also lined up to see the inside of the statue. We had to wait for more than an hour before it was our turn to climb the stairs that lead to her crown. We didn't mind; we were looking forward to the view from the top.

At first, the steps inside the statue were low and wide and we climbed slowly as the crowd packed in behind us. As we ascended, I noticed a big sign that said: "Do not climb stairs if you have any physical limitations." But the stairs seemed easy enough to me, and I knew I was in pretty good shape from playing tennis, so I ignored the sign and plunged ahead. Unfortunately, about half way up the statue, the spiral staircase narrowed considerably and the stairs themselves became very steep. They were so steep, in fact, that there wasn't enough room for me to lift my artificial leg from one step to the next. The ankle on my artificial leg doesn't bend and it was impossible for me in such a short, tight space to get my leg up to the next step.

"Donna," I said. "I'm stuck. We'll have to go back down."

Donna looked back. "We can't. There are hundreds of people jammed onto the stairs right behind us."

I had visions of being stuck in Lady Liberty forever and the mob behind me was beginning to grow restless. I could hear people wondering out loud what the holdup was, as I tried to figure out what to do next. Donna tried to lift my leg up, but she couldn't get it up over the steps, either. I had only one choice. I climbed the rest of the stairs in the Statue of Liberty on my hands and knees.

After what seemed like an eternity, I finally made it to the landing at the top of the statue. An elderly couple had been climbing just in front of us and the man became concerned when he saw me climbing up the last few flights on my hands and knees.

"Are you all right?" he asked. "Do you have a heart problem? Are you having trouble breathing?"

"No, that's not it," I said. "The problem is I have an artificial leg and these steps are very difficult for me."

The fellow looked at me, then at my leg, then at the steep stairs leading back down the statue. He grinned and took his wife's hand. Then he said to me:

"You don't mind if we get a head start, do you?"

He laughed so hard at his own joke he started coughing and the people behind us starting laughing, too. Pretty soon the entire inside of Lady Liberty was echoing with laughter.

❧

Once in awhile I get to turn the tables, though. For instance, when I travel, I often take along an extra leg or two just in case I need it. If I'm going to play tennis, I have to bring along my running leg and often I bring an artificial leg along to show during my presentations. I usually put them in my carry-on bag so I can keep them with me on the airplane. Of course, these bags have to go through the x-ray machines in the airport.

If I'm not in a hurry, I like to watch the looks on the x-ray attendants' faces as they check the contents of my bag. They've been watching cosmetic cases and cameras and other typical stuff all day long, then suddenly, two legs go by! It can lead to some quizzical expressions.

Traveling as much as I do can be wearing. The hardest part of it is being away from Donna so much, (although she does go on about half my trips). But when I'm by myself, it can be difficult to go to a strange city and give a presentation in front of thousands of people, shake scores of hands, then go back to the hotel and eat dinner alone. I don't like eating at restaurants or going out alone so I'm very thankful for room service and ESPN.

I've met some terrific people during my travels. I think my physical differences often make it easier for some people to talk to me. I try to be upfront about my handicap and that puts people at ease to be upfront about theirs. The result is a non-judgmental atmosphere that often nurtures the growth of deep and important friendships, even with people I've known only for a short time.

My experiences on the road have also under-scored my understanding of how many misunderstand-ings there are about handicapped people in this coun-try. For example, there is a common misconception that all handicapped people are either in a wheelchair or blind. A couple of times people have sent a wheel-chair to the airport to help me... even though they are aware that I am a professional tennis player. They sometimes reserve a handicapped-equipped hotel room for me. I always request another room because someone who needs these aids may want the room that night. I know my clients are just trying to take good care of me and I appreciate that, but their actions underscore the misunderstandings there are concern-ing physically challenged people.

Rental car company attendants often joke with me about driving one of their cars. They expect me to need some modifications to the car, even though I require none. (Although, since I've been known to get a ticket or two, Donna says they should put speed governors on the cars I rent.)

I remember a presentation I gave to a large par-ent teacher association at the Anaheim Convention

Center in Southern California. After my presentation, I fielded questions from the audience. One of the first questions was whether I had any brothers or sisters. I said I had a brother, Brian, and that we were regular brothers. We fought and he always won. Then, someone asked if Brian or my parents had any physical handicaps. I said no, but that like all people, sometimes they had a handicap from the neck up.

After the question and answer period was over, one lady came up to me with tears in her eyes. She told me I was a real inspiration to her—not only had I overcome my own physical handicap, but to think I had done it all in spite of having parents and a brother who were mentally handicapped. Mental and physical handicaps were so intertwined in her mind that she totally missed the point of what I was saying.

Americans annually spend billions of dollars on cosmetics and clothing in an effort to look different. I don't have to spend a thing. All I have to do is walk down a crowded mall or beach and I get more attention and stares than I could ever want. One thing I enjoy, especially in grocery stores and other public places, is to see how creative some people can be in their efforts to get a good look at my hands. I believe they think I don't notice, but a lot of times it reminds me of a spoof of some bad spy movie. I'll be walking along the vegetable aisle with them right behind me, peering over my shoulder. If I stop suddenly, they'll quickly grab the nearest cucumber or radish, and study it with intense interest.

Unless they are rude, I don't take offense at people who take an interest in my hands. I believe that, for the most part, they are just curious. I know when I see someone on the street who looks different, I also look twice. It's human nature.

The word *handicapped* was coined in the early days in England, when people with visible physical problems were turned out by society and had to beg along roadways. Most of them held out their caps in their hands. They were referred to as *hand-in-caps*, which was modernized to *handicapped*.

People ask me if the term offends me, and if it does, what is the preferred word. Frankly, I don't believe the term is that important, although I don't really like the word "disabled." It's a fine word to use around people who have physical limitations, but I think that when you say it to someone who doesn't really understand physically challenged people, they tend to equate "disabled" with "unable."

If I had to choose a description, I would say, "physically inconvenienced," comes close to describing the situation, but that's somewhat cumbersome. Until a better term comes along, I think "physically handicapped" or "physically challenged" are adequate.

Ironically, it isn't the words a person uses that tells me whether they accept me or not — it's the way they shake my hand. I always offer my hand when I first meet someone. Lots of people grab my hand and shake it firmly and I know they can deal with my handicap. But others will barely touch me, or they'll grab me around the elbow. That's a pretty good sign that they are very uncomfortable with my handicap. To put them at ease, I try to look them in the eye and smile. Smiling is a universal language; nothing puts a person at ease faster than a sincere smile. But regardless of what I do, there are some people who will never be comfortable around me. My hands and my leg are too much of a reminder of the frailty of the human condition and of their own mortality. I understand that and I also realize that the problem between us isn't my handicap, it's theirs.

One thing I would like to stress to able-bodied people who may be encountering a physically challenged person for the first time, is this: If you're curious, it's perfectly okay to ask them about their handicap. If that person takes offense at that, then that is really their problem. Asking questions about a person's physical handicap is not bad manners, or in bad taste. I welcome such questions because once they are answered, then we can take the next step in our relationship. I've had conversations with people for more than an hour before they confess what they really want to know is how my hands got the way they are. If you're curious, ask. Actually, I find the topic of my hands a good social icebreaker. Once people find out about them, they feel like they know me a little better and are more willing to open up about themselves.

One of my favorite groups of people to talk to is senior citizens. Most of them are very open-minded, energetic, and creative. I've always related well to senior citizens; I see in them a lot of wisdom and untapped potential. Too many people feel that when you reach a certain age you no longer have talents to tap, but that isn't true. Older people have a wonderful reservoir of experience to draw upon and that makes them some of the most interesting and vital people in our society. I've seen so many older people who are continuing to grow. I've taught groups of 70-year-olds, who were taking up tennis for the first time. I've talked to others who have discovered the joys of jogging, or the mysteries of classic books, or who have begun to travel for the first time in their lives.

In fact, one of my favorite stories comes from an experience I had at a senior home.

I talk a lot about building a positive attitude to older people and I find they really relate to that idea. It's as though the more life experience one has, the clearer it becomes that a positive outlook is the key that unlocks the door to a life of fulfillment. I had just finished one of my presentations in Richmond, California, when an elderly lady came up to me and put her hand on my face.

"Roger, I loved your talk, you're a wonderful young man. Don't you quit what you're doing because I believe in having a positive attitude, too. I'm 90 years old and I'm going to remember what you said today for a long, long time."

Chapter Seventeen

The Luckiest Man in the World

"Carrying the Olympic torch in the 1984 Olympic Games in Los Angeles was flat out the greatest thrill of my life."— Rafer Johnson, winner of the silver and gold medals in the decathlon in the 1956 and 1960 Olympic Games.

It might seem strange that Rafer Johnson, who won dozens of honors and two Olympic medals, would call carrying the Olympic torch his greatest thrill. But in a modest way, I know what he means.

The torch embodies the Olympic spirit of competition and international cooperation. Like the Statue of Liberty, it is a tremendously powerful symbol of hope and good will. Traditionally, runners have been chosen to carry the Olympic flame from the birthplace of the ancient games (Athens, Greece) to wherever the games are being held.

In 1984, the games were held in Los Angeles and the flame was transported from Athens to New York. Runners carried it by foot across the United States to the Los Angeles Coliseum, where Rafer Johnson used it to light the huge Olympic fire that burned throughout the games. Most runners along the way had corporate sponsors and most of the money raised was given to charities. I was lucky enough to be asked to carry the flame on part of its journey through northern California.

Radio station KFRC in San Francisco sponsored my portion of the run — I was to carry the torch through the heart of San Francisco, through Union Square to Chinatown.

I was excited because the media buildup had been unbelievable. I was interviewed by most of the local television news and radio stations, including one film crew that was shooting a documentary about the odyssey of the Olympic flame.

The weather on the day of the run was spectacular — the famous San Francisco fog was nowhere in sight, it was about 65 degrees, the Bay was still, and the sky was a deep turquoise.

A runner brought the flame up O'Farrell Street and I lifted my torch to hers. When my torch burst into flame, my heart jumped into my throat and I started in a sprint toward Union Square. It is hard to describe all the feelings I had as I ran through the throngs of people that were lining Post Street. It was just past noon and most of the people in the surrounding offices were on lunch hour and they were cheering and shouting encouragement as I ran by. The excitement that the torch created was tremendous. We all felt that it made us a part of the Olympic Games. Moreover, since the games were being held on American soil, everyone was feeling a swell of patriotic pride.

I climbed the last hill on Post Street and entered

Union Square, where the sight was so incredible I almost stopped in my tracks. The entire square was festooned in American flags and bright banners and streamers and thousands of people were standing in the park and along the sidewalks. The windows of the stately old St. Francis Hotel were underscored with red, white, and blue crepe paper and people were leaning out the windows and cheering. The 1984 Democratic Convention was being held in San Francisco and the Democrats were holding a rally in Union Square as I entered. Jesse Jackson was addressing the crowd. When he saw me, he stopped speaking and began to clap. The crowd turned and when they saw the torch, a roar went up that could have registered on the Richter scale. People lined the street 15 deep and many of them leaned over to touch the torch and to pat me on the back.

"Way to go! God Bless America!" people were yelling in unabashed enthusiasm. Many of them were crying and I started crying, too, which wasn't a smart thing to do because I couldn't see where I was going. I just followed the truck carrying the documentary camera crew and hoped it wouldn't make a wrong turn.

The truck led me through Union Square and we turned up Grant Street toward Chinatown. Grant Street, like most streets in San Francisco, runs up and down across the hills like a roller coaster. Unfortunately, from Union Square to Chinatown, there are a lot more ups than downs. Halfway up one steep hill my arms started getting tired. The torch, which was full of propane, was getting heavy. Most of the athletes carried it in one hand, but since I couldn't grasp it, I had to hold it with both hands, which made it difficult to run the hills. As I struggled toward Chinatown, the torch began to slip slowly through my hands — and the flame kept getting closer and closer to my hair. Before long, I got very nervous and started sweating, which made things worse because the torch got more slippery.

I would have given anything to stop and rest and get a new grip on the torch, but by now I was in the middle of a motorcade of television crews. Stopping was out of the question. As I made my way toward Chinatown, I began to wonder whether I was going to make it. My arm and leg muscles were cramping with pain and I still had several hundred yards to go. The flame was inching toward my hair and the thought went through my mind that I was about to become the first human Olympic torch in history. Just in the nick of time, I saw my mother and father ahead in the crowd. Somehow, they had struggled through all the people to meet me. Seeing them gave me a shot of adrenaline and took my mind off my problems with the torch. When I saw Dad put his hands together over his head in a victory signal, I knew everything was going to be all right. Holding the torch up as high as I could, I ran through the narrow streets of Chinatown and passed the flame on to the next waiting runner. Then I collapsed on the curb and gulped air. Mike Cleary, from radio station KNBR, came over to interview me, but he had to wait a few minutes until I could catch my breath.

Although the flame was passed on, I got to keep the torch I had carried. As I walked through the crowd, I was amazed at how many people wanted to touch and hold it. Later, when my parents and I were having lunch at the Golden Dragon Restaurant in Chinatown, an elderly Chinese couple came up to me and asked in broken English if they could see it. I handed it to them and they both put their lips to the crown and kissed it.

I'll never forget watching on television as Rafer Johnson climbed the steep steps of the Los Angeles Coliseum with the Olympic torch to light the huge Olympic flame signifying the opening of the games. After he lit the flame, he turned, lifted his torch high in the air and instantaneously the 100,000 people in the coliseum came to their feet and roared their approval. I can understand why he called that his greatest moment. But I'll also always remember those two Chinese immigrants who overcame their shyness to ask to hold the torch I had carried. Next to getting married, it was for me, as Rafer said, "Flat out, the greatest thrill of my life."

❧

I often think about how different my life could have been, had circumstances been different. What would I be like if I hadn't had parents who loved me, and who hadn't had the courage to mainstream me at an early age? What would I be like if I hadn't met people like Tony Fisher, whose patience and know-how helped turn me into a decent tennis player? What if I hadn't had the gentle guidance of teachers like Mr. Cross? Who would I be?

One day, in 1984, just as I was beginning my speaking career, I unexpectedly got an answer to some of those questions. I was still living in Los

Angeles and I had been speaking in front of a lot of university and high school groups, when I received a letter from a man who said he had heard me speak and would like to meet me in person. He lived on the coast, about 150 miles north of Los Angeles. He wanted to have lunch.

It was a nice, friendly letter so I waited until I had a free weekend and agreed to meet him at a restaurant near Santa Barbara. I was driving north on Highway 101, enjoying the spectacular view of the Pacific Ocean, when I realized that he hadn't told me what he looked like. But that has never been a problem for me when I am meeting someone in a restaurant or hotel lobby.

I found the restaurant, parked my car, and walked in. A man was sitting at the bar watching me as I came in. He slipped off his bar stool and walked over and introduced himself as the man who had written me the letter. He was tall, had a pleasant face, and he kept his hands in his pockets. I held out my hand to greet him. I noticed some reluctance on his part as he pulled his hand out of his pocket. When I saw his hand, I understood why. It was exactly like mine! In fact, both of his hands were malformed, though his legs were normal. I had never before seen anyone else whose hands were like that; I was so shocked that I couldn't say a word. It was like looking into a mirror.

After the hostess showed us to our table, we sat and began to talk. It was evident from the beginning that this man was very bitter about his handicap. He told me story after story about how the government refused to help him and how employers never gave him a chance. He was in his thirties and was living at home with his parents. He had never held a job for long and he complained bitterly that none of his relationships with women had worked out. He was sure that all of them had dumped him because of his hands. He was very angry and I didn't think it would do any good to confront him with the truth—which was that he would never find anyone to fall in love with him because he didn't love, or even like, himself.

I was never sure why he wanted to talk to me. It was obvious he didn't want to become friends because he was very hostile. Perhaps he thought I would understand his bitterness and sympathize with him. But I made it clear from the beginning that I wasn't there so we could feel sorry for ourselves.

It didn't take long to figure out the source of his poor attitude. He said his parents had always told him he would have difficulty competing in the able-bodied world. They sheltered him as much as they could. They kept him away from the pain caused by the taunts of the other kids, but also away from the challenges and experiences he needed to have in order to gain self confidence. At home, he became totally dependent on his family and he grew increasingly bitter. Here was a guy who was tall, not unattractive, and certainly not stupid. He could have made a great success of his life, but he lacked one vital thing—a positive self image.

As I was driving back home, I began to think of the things that separated his life from mine. I thought about my dad, who had the courage to have my leg amputated so I could run for the first time and who loved me enough to be tough; and about my mother, whose endless nurturing kept me going during the darkest times. And I thought about Tony Fisher, who took a little kid who couldn't even hit a tennis ball back over the net and taught him how to be winner. (And, of course, later on I found Donna!)

It wasn't long before my depression lifted and I began to get excited about getting home. The sun was going down over the Pacific and one last ribbon of gold light slanted in from the horizon. As I watched it glimmer, I felt I was the luckiest man in the world.

Roger Crawford is an internationally sought-after keynote speaker and consultant. He has delivered more than 3,000 presentations for Fortune 500 companies, national and state associations, and school districts. Roger is the recipient of the CPAE, a lifetime award and the highest award for speaking excellence and professionalism bestowed by the National Speakers Association. He is also a member of the illustrious Speakers Roundtable, whose membership includes 20 of the most popular speakers in the world.

If you would like to receive information on Roger's speeches, please write to:

Crawford & Associates
5658 Oakmont Court
Discovery Bay, CA 94514